Summer Vacation

Thanks to Adam, Meisha, Charlotte, Charley, Amy, John, Charlie, Pip, C. Vincent and Kathryn. Thanks to Sarah, for letting us use Cloud (Rufus), and to Talland School of Equitation, for letting us use their premises and horses.

© Eli B. Toresen/Stabenfeldt 2009
© Photos: Bob Langrish
Translator: Osa K. Bondhus
Repro: Italgraf Media
Printed in Italy, 2009
Editor: Bobbie Chase

ISBN: 978-1-934983-34-8

Stabenfeldt, Inc.
225 Park Avenue South
New York, NY 10003
www.pony4kids.com

Summer Vacation

By R.E. Toresen

Photos by Bob Langrish
Translated by Osa K. Bondhus

Chapter 1
Summer Vacation

Lynn raced up the driveway toward the farm, her unruly hair bouncing around her ears and her eyes beaming with excitement.

"Mum!" she yelled. "I'm home! What time is it? Do I have time to go to the stable before we leave?"

She flung the front door open as she talked. Two seconds later she landed on her back with a thump while a panting, dark bundle of fur jumped all over her. A wet, pink tongue licked her face delightedly.

"Rufus!" said Lynn, laughing. "Stop it, you silly dog!"

She pushed the excited dog off of her and stood up as her mother came out to the entrance to see what the commotion was.

"Goodness," her mum commented with a headshake. "I thought at least there was a murder taking place out here."

"Thanks all the same," Lynn exclaimed. "I think we're all good on murders around here as it is. You wouldn't even notice if the house collapsed around you when you're concocting one of your new, horrific crime plots."

Lynn's mum, Joanna, was an author who wrote somewhat bloodcurdling mystery novels. They sold well, but personally Lynn wasn't too fond of them. It would be much more exciting, she thought, if her mum wrote horse books, because horses were the best things in the world as far as Lynn was concerned.

Lynn's father, David, worked on an oil rig in the North Sea, not that far off the coast from where they lived in England. He was coming home the next day, and then he would be off for the next three weeks.

"By the way, what were you saying before this monster attacked you?" her mum asked.

"I was asking if I have time to go to the stable before we pick up Maria."

Joanna glanced at her watch. "Sure, but don't be long. No more than ten minutes! The ferry arrives in less than an hour, and it takes at least 20 minutes to drive to the ferry dock. And I'll need your help to hook up the horse trailer. I'm not used to doing it. Your dad is always the one who takes care of those practical matters."

"All right," said Lynn. "I'll be faster than

light. "Come on, Rufus! Let's go and give Golden Boy a treat."

She shouldn't have said that. As soon as Rufus heard the word "treat" he sat down right in front of Lynn with his paw up and two velvety brown eyes looking, pleading, straight at her.

"Ugh, you're so spoiled!" Lynn sighed. "Here, take this caramel, so at least I won't be the one to get cavities from it."

No sooner had she said it than the insatiable dog devoured the caramel.

"You could at least have taken the time to remove the wrapper," Lynn smiled in resignation as she stroked Rufus on the head. "C'mon, let's get going."

With the dog in tow, she ran across the farmyard and over to the stable. The stable was actually an old barn, but her dad had rebuilt the entire first floor and made seven horse stalls, a feed room and a saddle room. Currently he was leasing out four of the stalls. As soon as Lynn put her hand on the door to the stable, she was greeted by a chorus of neighing. She hurried into the cozy, warm stable.

"Hello there," she said softly to the five horses, who were all sticking their heads over their stall doors. "I'll come back and talk to you guys later. I don't have time right now. But I do have a little treat for you," she whispered to Golden Boy. "Let's just hope the others don't get jealous."

Lynn had gone over to the stall where Golden Boy was standing. He was Lynn's horse, a beautiful, golden gelding with a cream-colored mane and tail. He was supposed to have been a racehorse, like his mother. She was a renowned warm-blooded racehorse named Lizabona, and his father was supposed to have been the equally famous racehorse, Stardust. Things didn't exactly go according to plan, however, as such things often don't. A Haflinger stallion in the neighborhood escaped from his pasture one day and decided to pay Lizabona a visit, and the result was Golden Boy. He was the spitting image of his father, and everyone who saw him thought he was a full-blooded Haflinger. Golden Boy developed into a typical riding horse with absolutely zero talent for racing. David, who knew the owner, was able to buy Golden Boy at a very good price. It turned out to be a purchase that neither he nor Lynn had ever regretted. Golden Boy was as gentle as a lamb and very eager to learn. He was now five years old, and Lynn had only one problem with him; he was scared to death of white plastic bags. Every time he spotted a white bag on the side of the road, or anywhere else, he totally freaked out. Lynn had tried everything she could think of to help him overcome his phobia, but it was no use. White plastic bags were very, very scary, and that was that.

Lynn put her arms around Golden Boy's neck and rubbed her cheeks against his soft coat.

"You know what?" she said. "Maria is coming today."

Maria was an only child, just like Lynn, and the two girls had been best friends since before Maria moved to the Netherlands.

"She's going to stay with us for the entire summer vacation, and she's bringing her pony with her too! They'll be arriving on the boat in a little while. We're going to have so much fun this summer! Just imagine! We can go riding, and swimming, and riding, and – Oh, I'm so excited, I can't wait!"

Golden Boy let out a low neigh, as if he wanted to say that he was looking forward to it too.

"Lynn! Did you fall asleep in there?" It was her mother's voice. "Will you please come and help me with this blasted horse trailer? I can't figure out which connection goes where!"

"Coming!" Lynn gave Golden Boy the juicy apple pieces she had brought for him, then stroked him lovingly on the muzzle and hurried outside. Rufus jumped along beside her, wagging his tail excitedly.

Ten minutes later, Lynn and her mother were on their way to pick up Maria and her horse. In the back seat sat Rufus, panting happily. Lynn had tried to shut him in the kitchen, but Rufus had no intention of going along with that idea. Before she knew it, he had bolted past her, out the door, and jumped into the car. He looked quite triumphant and refused to budge. Nothing was more fun to Rufus than going for a ride in the car. Lynn tried threats and treats to get him out of there, but eventually she had to give up and let him come along for the ride.

"I can't wait to see Maria again!" Lynn smiled. "It feels like it's been forever since I visited her in the Netherlands."

"It's certainly been forever... right!" replied Joanna sarcastically. "You were there at Easter, remember? It's only been a little over two months! But I know that you miss her. Your dad and I were sorry to see the Steemans move back to the Netherlands too. They were the nicest neighbors we've ever had."

Maria's dad was born and raised in the city of Alkmaar, in the suburbs of Amsterdam, which was where they lived now. Her dad had been offered a very good job with a big company there, and Maria, who was every bit as crazy about horses as Lynn, had become the happy owner of no less than two horses. When Lynn visited Maria, she got to ride Le Bel, a beautiful, dappled riding pony. It was this horse that Maria was bringing with her for the summer.

"Poor Friedrich. He didn't get to come!" said Lynn.

"Who's Friedrich? Is he Maria's boyfriend?" asked Joanna curiously.

"Boyfriend? Of course not!" Lynn gave an indignant snort. "Friedrich is Maria's racehorse, silly! Don't you remember I told you that Maria is doing really well in competitive show jumping? She needs a good jumping horse for that. Le Bel is great for leisure riding and gymkhanas, but Friedrich is a full-blooded racehorse with a mile-long pedigree. He cost over 50,000 dollars, but apparently that's not a problem for Maria's family nowadays. I'm glad Maria didn't get all stuck-up by being so wealthy."

"It'll be fun to see her again," said Joanna. "We're almost there."

A few minutes later they were standing on the ferry dock watching while the ferry was being maneuvered into place. Lynn thought it took an unusually long time, but finally the landing was lowered and people and cars started streaming out. After the worst rush was over, a funny-looking party appeared on the landing. Two men appeared first. They were walking backwards, pulling on something. That something proved to be a very reluctant pony. Behind the pony was a slender, little figure. She was pushing for dear life.

"Maria!" shouted Lynn excited. "Hi, Maria! I'll help you!"

She ran across the landing and stood next to Maria. "What's the matter with Le Bel?"

"I'll tell you later, if I can just get him out of here!" said Maria, panting.

The girls pushed and the men pulled, and at long last the poor pony was standing on the dock, all sweaty and trembling.

"It was a mouse!" explained Maria, after she had said a proper hello to Lynn and Joanna. "It was inside the transport box on the boat. And Le Bel happens to be scared to death of mice. Some crewmembers managed to get the mouse out of the box, but it was too late. By then, Le Bel was beside himself with fear. I've been sitting inside that stupid box the entire trip, trying to calm him down. He did calm down after a while, but when it was time to get off the ferry he acted like he was seeing mice everywhere. He stood there like a rock and refused to move! That's why I had to get those guys to help me unload him."

"Poor little Le Bel," said Lynn and stroked the horse soothingly on the muzzle. "No need to be scared anymore. Fortunately we've got plenty of cats in our neighborhood, so there are no mice in our stable."

"Woof! Woof!" Barks suddenly erupted behind them. It was Rufus, tired of waiting. He was hanging halfway out the side window of the car, making himself look as cute as he could to Maria. She went over and petted him, and Rufus fluttered with delight.

"Le Bel isn't scared of dogs, I hope?" Joanna looked at Maria with a worried expression.

"No, he's not. We have a cocker spaniel at home, and Daddy's talking about getting a guard dog. You see, we had intruders in the stable just a few nights ago."

"Really? How scary!" Lynn exclaimed. "Did anything get stolen?"

"No, fortunately not. The police thought the thieves might have been scared off by something, but I'm pretty sure it was Friedrich they were after. He's pretty valuable, as you know. Anyway, the police are going to keep an eye on the stable for a few nights, just in case they try again. It would

be terrible if Friedrich were stolen, not just because of his monetary value, but because I love him! Almost as much as Le Bel."

While they had stood around talking, Maria's luggage had been carried ashore.

"Goodness gracious!" Joanna exclaimed.

"Good thing I have a big car! What in the world is all that stuff?"

"Oh, this? Just some clothes, plus Le Bel's saddle and bridle and grooming tools and horse cover and health supplies and bandages and –"

"All right, all right, I get it!!" Joanna raised her hands to stop her. "Lynn and I will load it into the car while you put Le Bel in the trailer. No mice, guaranteed!"

They all laughed. None of them noticed the man who was standing between some containers and watching them as they loaded everything into the car. When they were finally done and getting ready to drive home, he hurried over to a blue VW Golf, started the engine and turned onto the main road a little behind them. He kept a safe distance, and when they turned into the driveway in front of the cozy, little white house, he drove past the property and parked among some trees, out of sight from the farm. He fished out a cell phone and sent a text message. Then he waited...

Chapter 2
Attempted Burglary

It was late when Lynn and Maria finally fell asleep that night. They had so much to talk about.

"How about a nice, long horseback ride tomorrow?" suggested Maria. "Le Bel could sure use it after that long boat ride. It's funny how fast he settled into his new stall. Frankly, I had expected him to make a fuss about it, but he was as gentle as a lamb out there. And there was nothing wrong with his appetite either!"

Lynn started giggling. "He must take after his owner!"

Maria was known to have a ravenous appetite.

"Meany!" Maria laughed and started a pillow fight.

When they eventually stopped, flushed and out of breath, Maria suddenly looked around the room and said, "Where did Rufus go, by the way? Is he sleeping in the kitchen?"

Lynn shook her head. "No, his fur is so thick, it's too hot for him inside in the summer. He starts panting and whining like crazy, making it impossible for anyone else to sleep. So Dad built him a dog house behind the stable."

It was quiet for a little while, then Lynn said, "I know what we can do tomorrow! How about riding up to Linden Lake and going swimming? We can ask Thea and Thomas to come along too. The water won't be very warm yet, but it doesn't matter. Or have you turned into such a big wimp down there in Alkmaar that you can only swim in a heated pool now?"

"Me, a wimp?" Maria yelled. "I'll show you wimp! Do you want to lose another pillow fight? How about I use you for my pillow?"

"Relax," said Lynn with a giggle. "Just kidding!"

"By the way, who are Thea and Thomas?" asked Maria.

"They're twins. And they're fourteen, just like us. Actually, they turned fourteen last month. We had a great birthday party for them at the stable. Even the horses got a birthday cake, their very own custom-made horse cake. It was a blast! The twins own two of the horses that you saw in the stalls next to the racehorses. The Appaloosa, whose name is Oscar, of all things, belongs to Thea. Thomas owns the warmblood mare, Cinderella's Dream, which we just call Cindy for short. They're really nice. You'll like them."

"Who?" teased Maria. "The twins or the horses?"

"All four, actually," Lynn answered. "Even though Oscar can be as stubborn as a mule sometimes. The twins moved here last fall. That's why you don't know them. They live in a townhouse over in the new subdivision, but since they're not allowed to keep livestock over there they're boarding the horses at our stable. Thomas isn't really all that interested in horses anymore. Can you believe that? He's been talking about selling Cindy. Apparently, it's too much trouble for him to have to come over here every day to exercise and take care of his horse."

"I can't fathom how anybody could get tired of horses!" said Maria emphatically. "That could never happen to me. I'm going to do show jumping until I'm at least a hundred!"

"If so, you'll probably make it into the Guinness Book of Records," yawned Lynn. "Gee, I'm really tired. Do you want to go to sleep?"

"Yeah, that sounds pretty good right now," mumbled Maria. "Good night. It'll be fun to go riding together tomorrow."

A little later they were both sound asleep. An hour passed... two hours... Then suddenly Maria woke with a start and sat up in bed. A dog was barking. It must be Rufus! The barking only got louder and louder, so Lynn woke up too.

"What's going on with Rufus?" she said, sounding surprised. "He doesn't ever bark in the night. We'd better go and take a look."

Hurriedly, the girls pulled on T-shirts and jeans. Then they ran down the stairs and almost knocked over Joanna, who was standing in the entrance, stepping into some boots.

"I'm sorry, did he wake up you too?" Joanna stood up. "I was just about to go out there and see what's going on."

As they stepped outside, Lynn thought she saw a dark figure disappear between the trees.

"Did you see that?" she exclaimed. "Somebody was running away really fast!"

"Don't be silly!" Her mum shook her head with a resigned look on her face. "I think you're letting your imagination run wild. What would anybody come around here for in the middle of the night?"

Just then, Rufus showed up. He wagged his tail and looked very proud of himself.

"Rufus, you bad dog!" Joanna scolded. "What are you doing, waking up people in the middle of the night? I thought the stable was on fire or something."

"Well, there may not have been a fire, but somebody definitely tried to break into the stable," said Lynn, who was standing in front of the stable door. "Come and see!

Somebody tried to unscrew one of the door hinges."

"You're right! I don't believe it!" shouted her mum after inspecting the door. "And look at this! The hoodlum broke a window, too! I'm sorry I accused you of letting your imagination run wild. I guess you did see a burglar! Unlucky for him, he didn't know how much of a ruckus Rufus was going to make. Was he planning to steal one of the horses, do you think? I guess he might have been after one of the racehorses... Or maybe he was just going to drug them, to make them not be able to race or something, or maybe –"

"Mum! Listen to yourself!" Lynn interrupted. "Now who's letting her imagination run

wild? Why would anybody bother to drug a racehorse that hasn't won a single race yet?"

"Oh... yeah, I guess you're right." Joanna smiled apologetically. "Must be the mystery writer in me working overtime. But don't you think that whoever it was must have been after one of the horses? Why else would they break into the stable? Good thing we have a solid lock on the door. If not, the burglar might have gotten away with whatever it was they wanted."

"Oh, no!" Maria suddenly burst out. "Is it possible that...?"

She stood there with a puzzled look on her face.

"Is what possible?" asked Lynn impatiently.

"Well, this is the second burglary attempt I've experience in the last couple of weeks. First one at home, and now another burglary attempt here. Do you think there could be a connection?"

Lynn and Joanna stared at her. Eventually Joanna said, "But, didn't you say they were after Friedrich? You didn't bring him here."

"We just assumed that it had to be Friedrich they were after, but what if it was Le Bel?" Maria shook her head, confused. "I just don't see why anyone would be interested in stealing a pony. It's not like he's very valuable or anything. Except to me, of course!"

"Oh well, there's no use standing here all night wondering about it," said Joanna. "Come on, girls, let's go back to bed. We can talk about this tomorrow when David gets home."

"But what if the thief comes back?" said Maria with a worried look. "What if he manages to get Le Bel out of here? I would die!"

"Don't worry," said Lynn. "No slimy thief is going to take any horse away from here! Rufus can stay in the stable for the rest of the night. Right, Mum?"

Her mum nodded in agreement. "He's a great burglar alarm. Even though he wouldn't hurt a fly, the thief doesn't know that. What do you think, Maria?"

Maria looked more relieved as she answered, "I'll feel a little safer if Rufus stays in the stable."

It took the girls a while to wind down from all the excitement, but a little over an hour later they finally fell asleep again. Nobody except Rufus heard the stealthy footsteps approaching the stable. He started growling, quietly at first, then louder. The footsteps quickly went away again. A few minutes later, a car engine started up by the edge of the woods and drove away slowly.

Chapter 3
Trail Riding

"Hey! Maria! Wake up!"

"Hmmm...? What? Why?" mumbled Maria into her pillow. But the next moment she was wide awake. "Did the thief come back?"

"No, no – take it easy!" laughed Lynn. "But look at the time. It's nine fifteen. We were supposed to go on a long ride today, remember?"

Maria jumped out of bed. "Give me two minutes to shower and brush my teeth, and I'll be ready to go!"

"All right." Lynn went to the door. "I'll go downstairs and make us some bag lunches in the meantime. Mum's already been over to the stable. She fed the horses and let Rufus out of his prison."

Fifteen minutes later they were both outside, busy grooming the horses in the farmyard. The sun was shining from a clear sky, making it a rather sweaty job.

"Boo!" said a loud voice behind Lynn. She was so startled that she almost dropped the grooming brush. When she turned around, Thomas was standing there, grinning at her. Thea was with him.

"Hey, you scared me!" gasped Lynn. "I didn't hear you coming, until you roared in my ear." She put a hand over her heart, which was still thumping hard.

Thea shot her brother an irritated look. Why did he always have to be so childish?

Lynn caught her breath from the shock. "Maria, meet The Terrible Twins, Thea and Thomas," she said, then added to the twins, "Maria and I are riding up to Linden Lake today. Want to come? I just made a ton of sandwiches, and I'm sure we've got enough for everybody."

"I'd love to!" said Thea, excited. "A nice, long horseback ride is exactly what I need. But I don't know about Thomas. He's gotten pretty lazy lately. All he thinks about are girls and motorcycles!"

"So not true!" protested Thomas. "I think about food too!"

They all laughed.

"Actually, a nice, long ride would be perfect today," continued Thomas. "Because tomorrow I'm going on a camping trip with my buddies. We'll be gone for a whole week, so Cindy won't be getting any

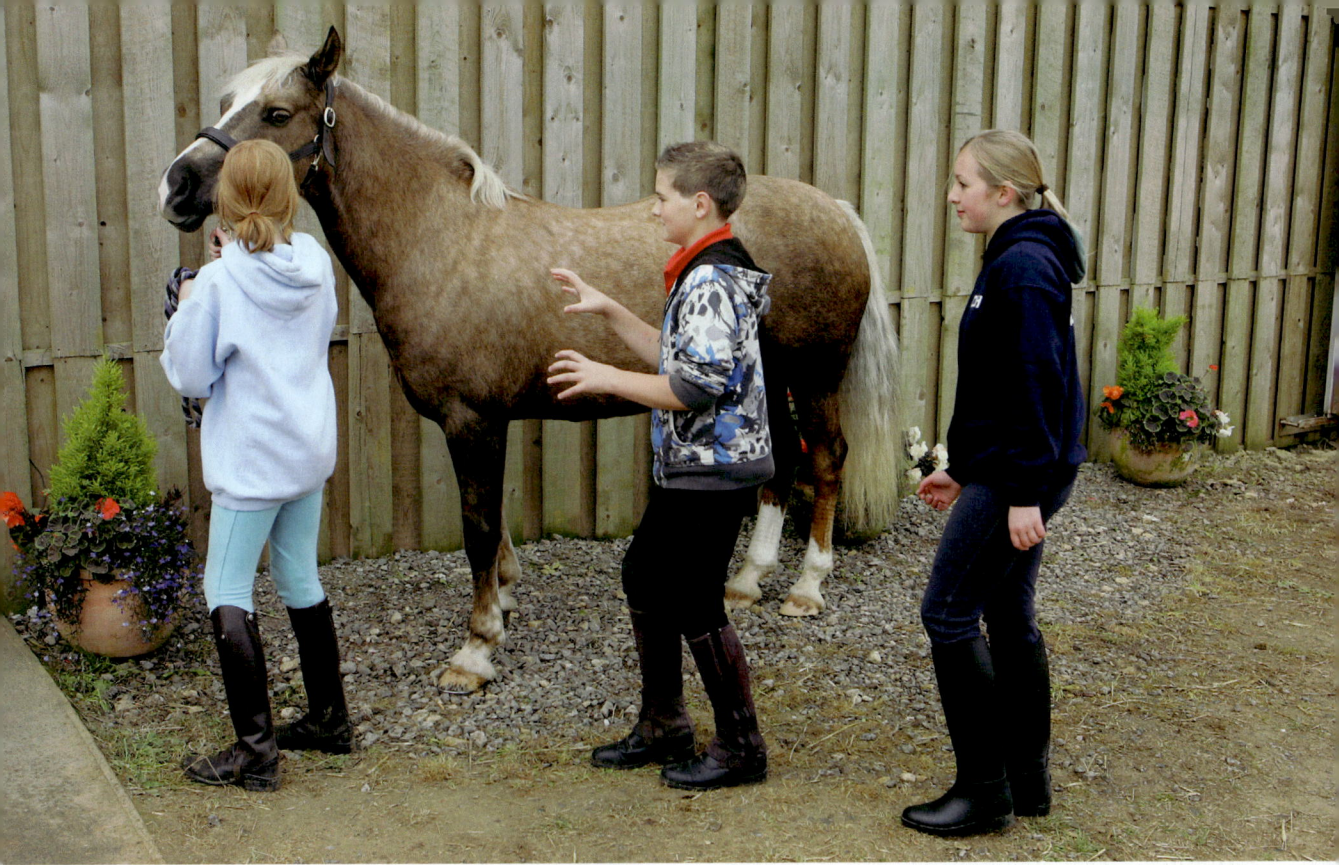

exercise for a while. I figured I could put her in the pasture while I'm gone. Do you think that'll be okay, Lynn?"

Lynn nodded. "I'm sure it will be. If you're not worried about her getting stolen, that is. We had some horse thieves visiting here last night."

"Yeah, right!" Thomas laughed out loud. "You didn't see Santa too, did you?"

"It's true!" said Maria. "But we think that the thief, whoever he is, is after my pony, Le Bel. I just don't know why."

Maria and Lynn had to explain the whole story about the break-in at Maria's place in Alkmaar and the attempted break-in last night while they all got their horses ready. Oscar evidently felt like he was not getting nearly enough attention, because he snorted angrily several times and tried his best to nip at anyone who came his way. When he finally managed a bull's eye on Thea's behind, he neighed so delightedly that they couldn't help laughing.

"What a spoiled brat you are!" Thea exclaimed. "Can't you see that we have important and interesting matters to discuss?"

But no, Oscar definitely didn't see that. Nothing could possibly be more important or interesting than taking care of him, he seemed to think.

"You're so darned cute, though!" Thea patted him on the neck. Oscar laid his head on her shoulder and looked as if he enjoyed being petted.

"Well, we'd better get our saddles and get going," said Lynn. "Will you stay with the horses while Thomas and I get the tack?"

Maria and Thea nodded. Lynn and Thomas had to make four trips back and forth before they had everything. Then they finally started saddling up the horses.

All of a sudden, Maria burst out, "What the –! Le Bel's saddle doesn't fit anymore! It's too wide. How weird..."

"Not that weird, really." Thea started laughing. "You see, that's Oscar's saddle you're holding. How cool is that? We've got the exact same type of saddle! I assume you bought yours in the Netherlands, right?"

"Yes, I did," answered Maria. "But what do we do now? We're bound to grab the wrong saddle every time we go riding, since they look exactly alike. Only the width is slightly different."

"No problem." Thomas smiled. "We'll just get a marker and put a small mark on one of them."

He turned Le Bel's saddle over. "Lynn, if you go and get a marker, I'll fix this in no time."

Lynn did as he said, and soon there was a big, red X on the underside of Le Bel's saddle.

"There!" Thomas said, all happy with himself. "If you guys have any other problems, just let me know. Thomas, the genius, will fix anything."

"Show-off!" Lynn dropped a handful of gravel on his head. "There, now you'll have to go swimming in the lake when we get there, no matter how cold it is."

"Guys! If you're all going to keep fooling

around, we'll never get there," complained Thea. "Get a move-on, will you?"

Finally they were all in the saddle and ready to go.

"Should we take the shortcut across the fields, or go through the woods?" asked Lynn.

"Personally, I'd like to ride through the woods." Maria looked at the others. "Where I live, there are barely any trees at all. And even though I do like Alkmaar, I have to admit I miss the different kinds of nature here in England."

"Then let's go through the woods," decided Thomas. "I'd better go first, since Cindy can't stand to have other horses in front of her. She seems to think she's the leader of the herd."

Maria rode next in line behind Thomas, then Lynn and Thea last. It was nice and cool and quiet in between the tall trees.

"Look!" said Thea suddenly. "That's a funny place to park a car."

She pointed at a blue VW Golf that was parked on a narrow dirt road.

"It's probably a jogger who likes to work out in nature," said Lynn. "Some people drive out of town and into the woods, where they can go jogging or hiking in the fresh air between bushes and trees. Can't say I blame them, either. Huffing and puffing on a treadmill next to a hundred other people at a gym doesn't sound like too much fun to me."

"Actually, I think the car might belong to the horse thief," declared Thomas, looking gravely at the others.

Maria's face turned white.

When Thomas saw that, he quickly said, "Relax! I was just kidding. I didn't mean to scare you. The horse thief is most likely long gone by now. He probably gave up when he realized that the stable is guarded by a fierce, dangerous dog."

"Yeah! Such a fierce and dangerous dog, oh my!" laughed Lynn. "Rufus is so sweet and gentle that at times he acts like a total doofus!"

"He can't be all that dumb," commented Thomas. "He managed to follow us."

Everyone turned around, and sure enough, there was Rufus, panting and

wagging his tail. His tongue was dangling out of his mouth like a pink tie.

"How did that happen...?" wondered Lynn. "I shut him inside the kitchen before we left."

"Well, he's not in the kitchen now," said Thea, somewhat needlessly. "But it doesn't matter if he comes with us, does it?"

"No, he deserves to be with us," said Maria, "as clever as he was last night."

So they continued riding. Rufus scuttled about happily, now in front, now in the back. The horses were perky and alert, walking ahead with eyes wide open and ears pointed.

"How about a quick race across the big clearing over there?" asked Maria.

"Sure, if you guys don't mind losing." Thomas grinned confidently. "Just be forewarned; Cindy is as fast as a speeding bullet. I'm afraid you guys won't stand a chance!"

"Wanna bet?" Lynn gave him a challenging look. "I bet a cheeseburger that Maria will beat your sorry self."

"You're on," said Thomas.

When they got to the clearing, they lined up all the horses. Then Thea shouted, "Ready, set... go!"

And the race was on. Thomas had an explosive start. Cindy really did take off like a bullet. Lynn and Golden Boy were second, but in no time Maria and Le Bel had caught up with them. They also gained steadily on Thomas and Cindy. Thomas saw the danger and urged Cindy on, but to no avail. Le Bel sailed past him in glorious style and reached the end of the clearing as the superior winner.

"What did I tell you, Thomas?" Lynn laughed triumphantly. "Yippee, you owe me a ..."

She suddenly fell silent. Running out from the trees, right in front of Golden Boy, came a figure dressed in a light purple T-shirt and shorts. Lynn pulled on the reins and used her leg aids in a desperate attempt at steering away, but it was too late. A collision could not be avoided. Lynn heard a sickening thump.

In the next moment, the purple-clad figure flew through the air and hit the ground with another thump. Lynn slid down from the saddle and rushed over to the person lying motionless on the ground. She could tell it was a girl about her own age. By now the others were running toward them. Just as they got there, the girl started moving. Then she sat up and looked around with a confused expression on her face. Lynn started crying in sheer relief.

"I thought you were dead," she stammered between sniffles. "I thought I'd killed you!"

The girl tried to smile, and as she did, Lynn, Thea and Thomas all recognized her at once.

"Monica!" they all exclaimed in unison.

"How are you feeling?" asked Thea. "Are you all right?"

"I... I think so," Monica stammered. "My hip and left arm are hurting, but I don't think anything's broken."

"See if you can stand up." Thomas reached a hand out to her. "I'll help you."

Monica stood up on shaky legs. "See? I'm all in one piece! It takes more than a horse to knock me out."

"But why did you run out right in front of the horse?" asked Maria. "Didn't you hear us coming?"

"No, I'm afraid I didn't," said Monica. "And I'll show you why. That is, if I can find that darned thing again! It must have flown through the air too, when the horse hit me. Or maybe I should say, when I hit the horse."

She started searching the ground, which was covered in long grass. "Aha! Here it is." She held up a thin, rectangular object.

"An MP3." Thomas said. "Well, now I understand why you didn't hear us."

"The worst part is that my mum's warned me repeatedly not to jog around with music in my ears," said Monica. "She says it's too dangerous in traffic, but I didn't count on too much traffic here in the woods."

Suddenly she started laughing. "I'm probably the only jogger who's ever been run over by a horse!" she gasped. "A horse has been at the top of my wish list for a long time now, but I didn't expect one to drop right into my lap."

And with that, all five of them burst out laughing. They laughed until they cried. Rufus, who hadn't understood much of all the commotion, was thrilled that suddenly everyone was so cheerful. He ran back and forth, barking and wagging his tail and was beside himself with delight. Neither he nor any of the others noticed the dark figure spying on them from behind a thicket in the woods.

Chapter 4
The Forest Has Many Eyes

Monica ended up going with the others up to Linden Lake. She didn't think there was much point in going home.

"Both my mum and my brother are at work, so I'd much rather go with you guys. If you don't think it's too much trouble to have me tag along, that is."

"Absolutely not. It'll be fun," said Lynn, and the others nodded in agreement. Everyone thought Monica seemed really nice. She was in the same grade and the same school as Thea, Thomas and Lynn. Monica and her brother, Steven, had moved to the area with their mother only six months ago.

Lynn had heard something about Steven being the reason they had decided to move to a different part of the country. Apparently he had gotten into trouble with the police, taking part in burglaries, car theft, vandalism and other illegal things. Lynn saw him frequently. He was eighteen, had dark, somewhat unruly hair, and was usually wearing old jeans and raggedy T-shirts. As soon as they'd moved here, he had gotten a job as an apprentice plumber or something like that, or so Lynn had been told.

Monica's mother was a dental hygienist and worked at the dental clinic in town.

"Hey! I can see the lake!" shouted Thomas, who was riding in front. Monica was riding double with Maria on Le Bel, holding on as best as she could.

Rufus, barking excitedly, ran right into the water and started swimming around in circles before the kids could even dismount.

"Poor dog, he must have been dying in this heat." Maria looked at the dog with sympathy. "I'm glad I don't have a thick fur coat like that."

They had just gotten down from the horses when Rufus came back to the shore. He ran right over to where they were standing and shook vigorously, spraying water all over them.

"Rufus! You monster!" squealed Maria. Then she laughed. "Talk about service. We don't even have to go into the lake to get wet. Rufus is giving us a free shower!"

"Well, I'm gonna go swimming no matter how cold the water is," said Monica. "I'm so hot, I'm dripping with sweat!"

They unsaddled the horses in a hurry and

tethered them under some trees, where they could graze in the shade. Then they changed into their swimsuits. Of course, Monica didn't have a swimsuit with her, but she didn't care. "I'll just swim in my T-shirt and shorts, then I'll get them washed at the same time," she said. "They'll probably dry in the sun in no time."

"Last one in is a rotten egg!" roared Thomas, and he ran toward the lake. Unfortunately for him, he was in such a hurry that he stumbled on a tree root and fell headfirst onto the ground. By the time he got to his feet, the others had already jumped in the water.

"Did you find something?" teased Lynn. "Like a rotten egg, maybe? C'mon in, slowpoke. The water feels great!"

"You just wait!" Thomas jumped in. Lynn swam as fast as she could, but he caught up with her in no time. Just as he was about to grab her and dunk her head under water, Rufus started barking up a storm back on the shore. He looked into the woods and barked like crazy. The next moment, he took off in between the trees and was gone, which brought a hush to the party.

"What's that dog doing now?" exclaimed Lynn.

"He probably gotten a whiff of some animal," said Thomas. "German Shepherds are hunting dogs, aren't they?"

"I have no idea," said Lynn. "But anyway, Rufus isn't a full-blooded German Shepherd, he's a mutt. Still, I find it hard to imagine him as a hunting dog. He's usually afraid of other animals. He's scared to death of sheep, for instance. Once he heard some sheep baaing on TV, and he ran right under the couch and hid."

"Maybe we should go and look for him," suggested Thea.

So they did, but all their searching and calling for him was to no use. Rufus was nowhere to be found. Lynn was on the verge of tears.

"Don't worry," said Thomas. "I know what we'll do. Let's sit and eat our lunch. I bet that'll bring him back in no time."

And sure enough, no sooner had they unwrapped their food than Rufus came bounding toward them.

"So that's how it goes, huh?" laughed Maria. "Couldn't resist the smell of food, could you?"

She held out a ham sandwich to Rufus, but he merely sniffed at it. Then he padded away and lay down in the shade of a tree where he stayed, stretching lazily and yawning widely.

"I don't believe it! That's the first time I've ever seen him turn down food," said Lynn with a frown. "Do you think he's sick?"

But Rufus didn't look sick, only full and very sleepy.

After they cleaned up their meal, Thomas looked at the others. "What should we do now?"

"Well, I know what I'd like to do," said

Monica somewhat shyly. "I'd give anything to ride on one of those horses."

"Do you know how to ride?" asked Lynn.

"Yes, I do. I went to a riding school for several years where we used to live, but I haven't ridden in a while. We pay so much rent at our new apartment complex that I haven't dared to ask my mum for riding lessons. But, it's the same with horseback riding as with riding a bike, isn't it? Once you've learned it, you don't really forget it?"

"Of course you can ride!" said Thea and Maria in unison.

"But just to be on the safe side, I don't think you should choose Oscar," added Thea, glancing at her horse. "He tends to be difficult with people he doesn't know. I think Cindy would be a better choice."

"I just got the greatest idea," said Thomas. "But I'm not gonna tell you what it is, until Monica has tried riding Cindy first."

Monica and Thomas walked over to Cindy. The mare turned around and looked at them with gentle, dark eyes. When Monica carefully reached her hand out toward her muzzle, Cindy sniffed curiously at Monica's fingers, as if she was looking for something.

"Sorry, girl, I don't have a treat for you right now." Monica stroked Cindy's warm, silky-soft muzzle. The horse neighed softly.

"She likes you," Thomas said happily. "That's good. Do you want me to help put her saddle on?"

"Thanks, but I can do it."

While Thomas watched, Monica placed Cindy's saddle on the mare's back and tightened the girth with rapid, experienced movements.

"Wow, you're quite the expert!" Thomas looked at her admiringly. "How's your hip feeling, by the way?"

"Not too bad. I might be a little black and blue for a few days, but oh well. It'll heal."

While Monica talked, she swung herself easily and elegantly up on Cindy's back and seated herself gently into the saddle.

"Would it be okay if I ride around in the woods for a little while?" she asked.

"Sure," replied Thomas. "The rest of us

will stay here and relax in the sun."

"C'mon Cindy, you and I are going for a stroll," whispered Monica softly into the horse's ear. She got a low snort for an answer, and Cindy started walking toward the woods.

Half an hour later, they returned. Monica's face was beaming.

"Cindy is wonderful!" she bragged. "Very sure-footed and gentle as a lamb, even though she clearly has some fire too. You are so lucky, Thomas. I wish she was mine!"

"Well, she could be, at least for a week." Thomas smiled. "That's what I wanted to talk to you about. I'm going on a camping trip tomorrow and I meant to leave Cindy in the pasture while I'm gone. If you'd like to borrow her for a week, though, nothing would make me happier."

"You mean it? Can I really borrow Cindy for a whole week? You're an angel!"

Monica threw her arms around Thomas's neck and gave him a big hug. Thomas got as red as a stoplight. To hide his embarrassment, he started fiddling with Cindy's bridle, but suddenly he noticed a prickly feeling down his spine, as if someone was staring at him. He glanced toward the woods. Did something just move in there? No, there was nothing now. He must have imagined it.

"I think I must have sunstroke or something," he said. "For a moment, I thought I saw somebody sneaking around in the bushes over there."

He pointed toward the edge of the woods.

Monica stared dumbfounded at him. Then she said slowly, "You know, I wasn't going to say anything, because I was sure I must have just imagined it, but when Cindy and I came back just now, I thought I caught a glimpse of somebody who quickly ducked behind those bushes over there."

They all started staring at the thicket, but nobody saw anything suspicious.

"Should we go over there and take a look?" said Thomas hesitantly.

"No!" Lynn exclaimed. "Let's not! I can't explain why, but I have a bad feeling about this. My gut tells me it might be dangerous. Let's get out of here as fast as we can."

Quickly, they packed their stuff, saddled up Golden Boy, Oscar and Le Bel, and set off for the stable. Monica rode Cindy as if she were a queen on her throne. Her cheeks were flushed and her eyes beaming. Not even an unexpected rain shower, which soaked them all to the skin, dampened her spirits.

Thomas ran next to Oscar, while Rufus scooted around in front of the group.

"Are you sure you don't want to ride double?" asked Maria. "Le Bel is strong enough to carry both of us, at least for a while."

"No, I had planned to go running tonight anyway," said Thomas. "This way, I won't have to. I'll be able to keep up as long as you don't start galloping!"

Maria giggled. A comical picture had flashed before her inner eye, of Thomas galloping, desperately trying to keep up with the rest of the field on a racetrack.

Lynn, who was bringing up the rear, turned and looked back several times, and didn't see anything but trees and bushes. Even so, she couldn't shake the unpleasant feeling she had. Who would have any interest in spying on them? And why?

No, it must have just been a figment of her imagination. She tried her best to convince herself, but didn't succeed.

Chapter 5
A Creepy Guy

Just as they rode into the farmyard in front of the stable, David walked out of the house.

"Hey guys!" he shouted. "How are you, Maria? It's nice to see you again. Did you all have a good ride?"

"Good and exciting," answered Lynn before Maria had a chance to say anything. "Dad, this is Monica," she continued. "She's going to borrow Cindy for a week, because Thomas is going camping."

"I see," said David. "I guess that explains why Thomas is on foot. I was wondering about that."

"We ran into Monica in the woods," Lynn went on. "Actually, Golden Boy ran into her, and pretty hard too, and afterwards we went swimming, and then Rufus disappeared, but he came back, and then somebody was spying on us, and..."

At this point, Lynn had to stop and take a breath. Her dad laughed and said, "Slow down, sweetheart! I'll be home for three weeks. You don't have to tell me a ten-minute story in ten seconds. Now, would you please back up a little? Did you say Golden Boy ran into Monica?"

After Lynn told the whole story, with a lot of help from the others, her dad said, "I can't say I like the sound of this. Joanna told me about the burglary attempt. It wouldn't surprise me if there's a connection, even though I can't figure out why somebody would go to all that trouble to steal an ordinary pony."

"Couldn't you call the police?" asked Lynn. "It would be good if they could keep an eye on the stable tonight."

"Yes, I'll call them," promised David. "But I highly doubt that they have time to keep watch at a stable. That's probably something we'll have to do ourselves. If Rufus stays in the stable, I bet the thief will keep away, though."

Just then, Joanna's head appeared in the kitchen window. "Lynn and Maria!" she shouted, "once you've put the horses in the stable, would you bike down to the supermarket and buy a couple of things for me?"

"Sure," answered Lynn. "Just write out a list."

Then they started grooming the horses.

That is, Lynn, Maria, Thea and Monica groomed and sweated. Thomas, on the other hand, got comfortable, lying down by the stable wall and watching them. Thea had problems getting Oscar to stand still. Her horse didn't like to be brushed at all, especially not under his tummy. It tickled! He stomped his hooves, snorted and threw his head up.

Thomas laughed out loud, which made Thea furious.

"It's not funny," she fumed. "Instead of just sitting around laughing, why don't you make yourself useful! You could muck out the stalls, since none of us had time to do it this morning."

All right, all right!" Thomas got up lazily. "Hold your fire! I'll muck, on one condition."

"And what's that?" Thea looked at him, suspiciously.

"That you wash Cindy's saddle and

bridle for me. I hate that job, rubbing and scrubbing with that awful saddle soap."

"I'll wash Cindy's saddle and bridle!" offered Monica instantly. "That's the least I can do when you're nice enough to let me use your horse for a whole week."

Golden Boy stood as if in a trance, thoroughly enjoying being brushed. Suddenly they heard a funny sound coming from him, and everyone looked up. Lynn started laughing.

"Did you hear that?" she said. "This horse is just standing here – snoring! It must be the heat. It wouldn't surprise me if we have a thunder storm tonight," she added. "It feels kind of foreboding with this humidity in the air, don't you think?"

Eventually they were all done working. The horses were happily installed in their own stalls with a generous helping of pellets, which Thomas had given them.

"There, now we can go to the store," said Maria. "Do you have a bike I can borrow?"

Lynn nodded. "You can take my mum's. Come on, let's go in and get the shopping list and money." She turned toward the others. "If you guys want to wait, we could go together as far as to the store."

"Okay, but hurry," said Thomas. "I want to go home and take a shower. I'm all sticky and sweaty."

When Lynn and Maria went inside, they heard David talking on the phone. "All right then," he said. "No, I understand. Yes, we'll do that."

He hung up and turned to the girls. "I talked to the police," he said. "They didn't seem overly interested and definitely have no time to keep an eye on a stable. They asked us to call if anything else happens."

"In that case, we'll have to trust Rufus to be a guard dog," sighed Lynn. "Unless you would consider letting Maria and me sleep in the stable?"

David shook his head. "That's out of the question! Rufus will do. He'll start barking and wake up the whole house if anybody tries to break in."

He sounded so determined that Lynn gave up the idea. She ran into the kitchen and got the shopping list and some money from her mother.

While they were all biking toward town Thea said, "You know what I'd like to do tomorrow? I'd like to make some hurdles and set up a jumping course in the clearing in the woods. You know, where we met Monica?"

Monica, who was riding on the bike with Thomas, replied excitedly, "That's a great idea! It's been years since I had a chance to jump! Is Cindy a good jumper, Thomas?"

Thomas shrugged his shoulders. "She's pretty average, I guess. She doesn't jump very high, but at least she likes it well enough. It's rare for her to resist."

"I'm turning fourteen on Saturday," said Monica. "Can you guess what's at the top of my wish list?"

"A moped!" suggested Thomas at once.

"Silly!" Monica laughed. "A horse, of course! But I have about the same chance of getting a horse as my brother has of getting a BMW. Steven just got his driver's license and has his heart set on a car of his own, but he can't afford one."

Monica got serious. "Unfortunately, we can't ask my dad for any money either. After he and my mum got divorced, Dad married his new girlfriend and moved in with her right away. She had two kids from before, and now they're expecting another one, so he's probably got less money than we do. He doesn't seem very interested in staying in touch with us, either. Apparently he's got more than enough with his new family. Steven didn't handle the divorce very well. That's when he started getting into trouble and hanging out with all the wrong people. He's on the right track again now, fortunately."

While Monica was talking, they reached the supermarket.

"See you later," said Lynn and Maria to the others. "And have fun on your camping trip, Thomas!"

Inside the supermarket was nice and cool. Lynn and Maria found what they needed and got in line at the cash register. Suddenly Lynn nudged Maria.

"See the guy second in line over there?"

Maria nodded.

"That's Steven, Monica's brother."

When it was Steven's turn to pay, a stocky, gray-haired man suddenly approached the cash register. "May I see what you have in your pockets, please?" he said, loud enough for everyone to hear it.

At first Steven blushed, then his face turned as white as a sheet. "It's none of your business what I have in my pockets," he said aggressively, but after a moment he turned out the pockets on both his jacket and jeans.

"Humph, all right!" said the gray-haired surly man, when they turned out to be empty. Then he turned abruptly and disappeared, without a word of apology.

"What a jerk!" exclaimed Maria when they were back outside. "Who was that?"

"That was D-i-r-e-c-t-o-r Olsen," answered Lynn, sarcastically. "That is, it used to be plain old Mr. Olsen before, when he was still just an ordinary, mortal storekeeper. But ever since he built this big supermarket, he's been so full of himself, it's ridiculous. He lives in that big, white mansion that we passed on our way here. Don't you remember, we met his son when I visited you last Easter?"

"Ohh... you mean that stupid, conceited guy with the new Mercedes? Sure, I remember him."

Lynn started thinking about the day when they had run into Martin in the Netherlands. She and Maria had gone into Amsterdam to do some shopping. They had just finished their shopping spree and were waiting for the bus home when a voice said, "Hi there! What are you doing out in the big, bad world, Lynn?"

When Lynn turned around, she looked straight into the face of Martin Olsen. He was sitting in the beautiful, gray car that his dad had given him for his 18th birthday.

"Hi, Martin!" she said, surprised. "What are you doing here?"

"Visiting friends." Martin smiled. "I met a lot of people on my InterRail trip last summer. Are you guys waiting for the bus?"

Lynn nodded. "We're going back to Alkmaar."

"I could drive you," offered Martin. "I have a couple of hours before I'm supposed to meet my friend, so I've got some time to kill anyway."

They got into the car, and soon they were tearing along. Martin liked to drive fast, and he liked to talk. He bragged nonstop about himself, his rich dad and his marvelous car. Lynn and Maria eventually got so fed up listening to his monologue that they regretted having taken him up on his offer. Finally Maria couldn't resist and said, "Personally, I don't really see what's so great about a car. I think a great riding horse is much better!"

"I see..." Martin smiled indulgently. "So you're one of those horse crazy girls! My sister was totally hooked on horses when she was younger, but fortunately she outgrew that nonsense. She lives in Paris now, studying Art History."

"Well, I'm never going to outgrow this 'nonsense,' as you call it," said Maria with conviction. "This summer I'm going to stay with Lynn, and I'll take one of my horses with me."

"That should be fun." Martin seemed interested all of a sudden. "You mean you have more than one horse?"

And for the rest of the trip, Martin asked a bunch of questions about Maria's horses, the stable and the equipment. Lynn figured he was just being polite.

"Hey, Lynn, wake up!" It was Maria talking, and Lynn was jerked back to the present. "Shouldn't we get home with these groceries now?"

Ten minutes later, they were sitting in Lynn's kitchen eating her mother's potato salad and yummy barbequed "summer chops," the pink-colored, smoked pork chops that Joanna knew they were Maria's favorites.

"Oh, I almost forgot," Joanna said suddenly. "Your mother called while you were at the store. She'll call again tomorrow."

"Anything new?" Maria asked eagerly. "No more burglaries, I hope?"

Joanna shook her head. "No, she said everything has been nice and quiet, but they're still guarding the stable, to be on the safe side."

After they were done eating, Lynn and Maria went out to the stable to say goodnight to the horses. Both of the stalls where the racehorses usually stayed were empty. The owner had picked up the horses and was taking them out of town. They were going to compete in a race in a neighboring county in the coming week.

Rufus scampered around the girls' feet.

"He won't be as happy when we shut him inside the stable again tonight," said Lynn. "Too bad Dad won't let us sleep out here. That would have been kind of fun, don't you think?"

"Yeah, I guess," said Maria, unconvinced. "But if there's a thunderstorm tonight, it'll be safer in the house. Besides, it's not very likely that the thief will come back. Maybe Rufus scared him away for good."

"Maybe," said Lynn. But for some reason she had a feeling that it wasn't over yet...

Chapter 6
Uninvited Guests

Late that night, the storm broke. The dark night sky was lit up by huge zigzags of lightning and the rumble of thunder filled the air.

"I'm never going to be able to sleep in this weather," uttered Maria miserably. "What if a lightning bolt strikes the house... or the stable?"

"Don't worry, Maria." David gave her a comforting smile. "Both the house and the barn have lightning rods on their roofs. So we're safe, people and horses."

They finally managed to calm Maria so she and Lynn could go to bed.

"But I won't be able to sleep, that much is certain," Maria stated. "However, that may be a good thing, because then I can listen for any suspicious sounds outside."

"Suspicious sounds?" Lynn chuckled. "With all this thunder, I doubt you'd hear anything even if a whole herd of elephants marched through the farmyard."

"I sure hope the weather will get nice by tomorrow," sighed Maria. "If not, it won't be much fun building a jumping course in the woods. Le Bel doesn't like being outside in rainy weather. It makes him kind of touchy and difficult."

"I'm sure the storm won't last very long," said Lynn. "It sounds like the thunder is going away already."

She was right. The storm gradually blew over and soon both Lynn and Maria were sound asleep.

In the stable all was calm and quiet. Both Rufus and the horses were sleeping when

a dark shadow quietly emerged from the woods and stealthily approached the farm...

The next morning, the girls woke early. Maria ran to the window and pushed the curtains open.

"Yippee!" she shouted. "The sun is shining. We're going to have a super-licious horse day!"

After quickly throwing on some clothes, they ran downstairs for breakfast. David was already sitting at the kitchen table drinking tea.

"Good morning, girls," he said. "Did you sleep well?"

"We slept like rocks," said Lynn. "Is Mum up yet?"

"Nope. She got this brilliant idea for a new mystery novel last night, so she sat up half the night writing. Don't think we'll see her smiling face for a few hours, if I know her."

Lynn laughed. "Where's Rufus, by the way?" she asked.

"Oh no!" David sighed. "He's still in the stable. I totally forgot about him! Bet he's not very happy right now."

"I'll go and let him out," offered Maria. "Then I can look in on Le Bel at the same time."

She picked up the stable door key, opened the front door and was almost run down by Rufus, who was jumping with morning happiness.

"Rufus!?" exclaimed Maria in surprise. "How did you get out of the stable?"

"Woof!" said Rufus, wagging his tail happily.

Lynn and her dad came out to the entrance, looking at Rufus, confused.

"Well, I certainly didn't let him out!" stated David firmly. "We'd better go and find out how this happened."

All three quickly stepped into their shoes and ran to the stable. When they got there they just stopped and stared. The door had been taken off its hinges and was dangling loose.

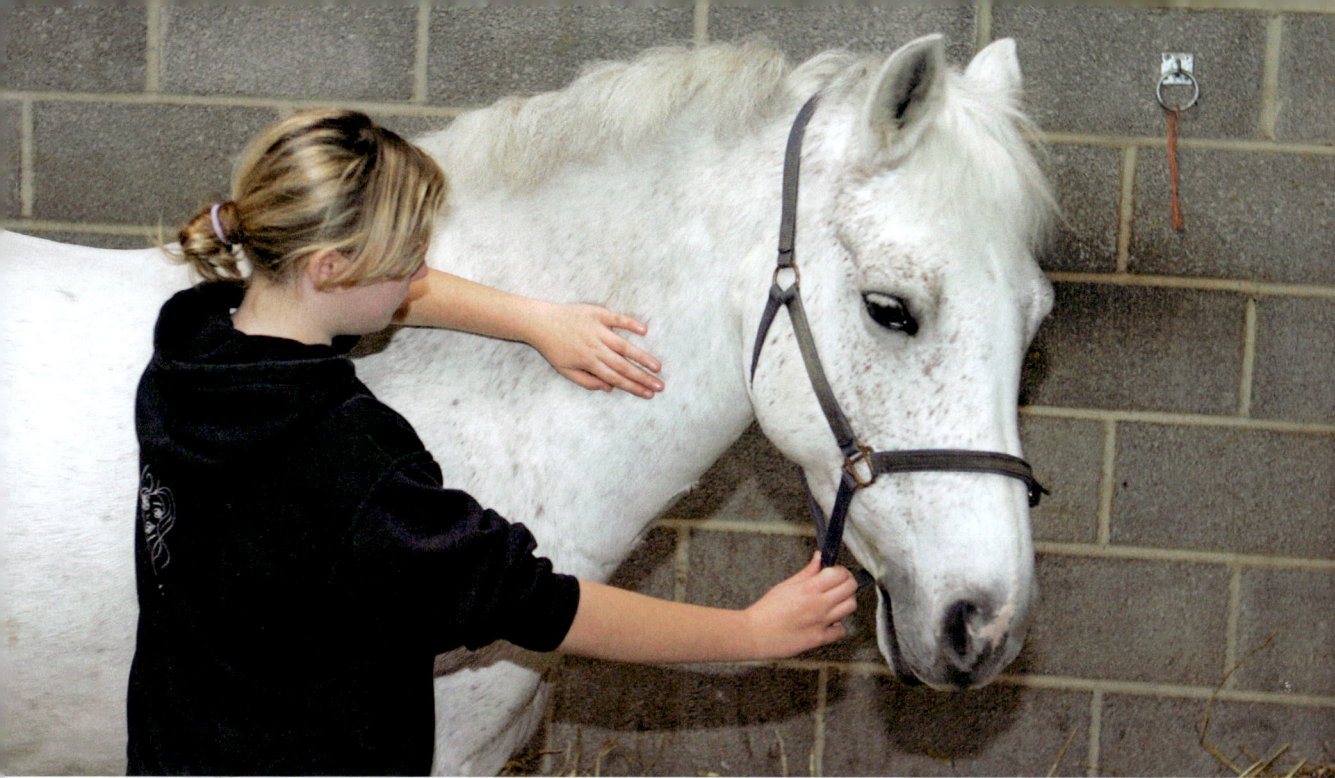

"Le Bel!" Maria stormed into the stable with the other two right on her heels.

They were met by four neighing voices. Golden Boy, Le Bel, Cindy and Oscar all looked at them, curiously. "What's all the fuss?" they seemed to be thinking.

"Oh, le Bel! I thought you'd be gone!"

Maria started crying in sheer relief. She threw her arms around Le Bel and her tears trickled into the horse's silky soft mane.

"Hello! What's going on? What happened to the stable door?"

Lynn turned and discovered Thea and Monica, who had just arrived. "We've had a burglary here!" she said dramatically. "Except, the funny thing is, nothing's been stolen. Le Bel is fine, and so are the other horses."

"Rufus must have scared them away before they could take anything," suggested Thea. "He kept guard in the stable last night, right?"

"Yes," said David, "but we didn't hear a peep from him all night. I don't understand why he didn't bark. The burglar must have worked a while to get those hinges loose."

"None of this makes any sense!" Lynn shook her head, resigned. "I'm just happy that none of the horses were taken. I can't help wondering why the thief gave up, though."

Maria looked at the others. "Do you think

they might have been after one of the race horses, and not Le Bel? I mean, since the race horses aren't here right now, that might be why the thief left without taking anything..."

"Well... I guess we can't rule it out, but frankly, I don't think it's very likely." David scratched his head. "Everyone who has anything to do with the horse community around here knows that there's an event going on this week. It seems kind of weird that a horse thief wouldn't have known that."

"So then we're back to Le Bel," Maria sighed. "If I could only think of a reason why anyone would be after my pony..."

None of them could offer her a good answer to that, and the horses started stomping impatiently inside their stalls. "What kind of nonsense is this? Aren't any of you going to feed us this morning?" Oscar seemed to say, clearly offended, tossing his head and neighing long and hard, making them all laugh.

"All right, you poor, starving thing! I get the hint," said Thea. "I'll feed you, don't worry!"

All four girls ran off to get an armful of hay, which they placed in the hay nets. Then they started grooming the horses. For once, Oscar stood still. He was so hungry that he didn't care if the grooming brush tickled a little.

"While you guys are taking care of the horses, I'll go inside and call the police," said David, and he left.

Suddenly Maria started crying again. She sniffled as she brushed.

"What's wrong?" Lynn asked, concerned.

"I feel so guilty," sniffled Maria. "There I was, sleeping safe and sound in my bed, without a thought to Le Bel's safety. I should have been sitting by the window keeping watch all night. If Le Bel had been stolen, it would have been my fault!"

"It would not!" protested Lynn. "We all thought the stable was well guarded. I can't imagine why Rufus didn't bark at all!"

She glared accusingly at Rufus, but he didn't seem to have the slightest bit of guilty conscience. He lay in the doorway and kept one eye on a big bumblebee that was buzzing around just outside the door.

Finally Maria calmed down and gave the others a timid smile. "I'm sorry for being so dramatic! It's stupid of me to carry on like this when all the horses are just fine!"

"Well, I refuse to let this ruin a perfect day for us," said Lynn, determined. "As soon as Maria and I have had something to eat, we'll ride out to the woods and set up hurdles just as we planned. Okay?"

The others willingly agreed. "Thea and I can muck out the stalls in the meantime," offered Monica.

Lynn and Maria hurried back to the house. Inside the kitchen, David had started doing the dishes.

"You called the police? What did they say?"

David shrugged his shoulders. "Yeah, I called. But since nothing was stolen, the police weren't really interested. They have more important things to do, I was told. There has been a rash of burglaries in our community lately, and apparently thieves are getting away with quite a lot of valuables."

"Does that mean we just have to sit here helplessly and wait until one of the horses is actually stolen?" asked Lynn with an offended snort.

"Not if I can help it," David said. "You can calm down. Tonight I'm going to keep watch in the stable myself. And that thief, whoever he is, had better watch out if he's planning any repeat visits!"

"Cool!" exclaimed Lynn excitedly. "Can we come too?"

David shook his head. "Absolutely not! You guys will sleep in the house, and that's that!"

Lynn looked dejected, but she gave up the idea.

When she and Maria went outside fifteen minutes later, Monica and Thea were waiting impatiently for them.

"C'mon, slowpokes," said Thea. "Let's get going!"

They went into the saddle room to get the tack for the horses. That's when they saw it. On the saddle bar hung three of the saddles just as they had left them, but the fourth space was empty!

"Oscar's saddle is gone!" exclaimed Lynn. "Or is it Le Bel's?"

"No, it's Oscar's saddle," said Maria.

"Look! This one has a big X underneath, so that's Le Bel's."

"I can't believe it!" Thea pulled on her hair. "Why on Earth would anyone break into the stable just to steal an ordinary old saddle?

"It seems totally ridiculous," Lynn chimed in. "You guys wait here while I go and get Daddy!"

She ran out the door. Two minutes later, she was back with her dad right behind her.

"See for yourself, Daddy!" she said, out of breath. "Thea's saddle is gone! You'd better call the police again. This time they can't refuse to come!"

Chapter 7
Suspicions

The girls waited in the farmyard as David went inside to call the police and report the new development. He came back out after a few minutes. "They'll be here some time this afternoon. You just go enjoy yourselves. I'll stay here and talk to them when they come."

"But we can't ride now that Oscar's saddle has been stolen!" said Lynn.

"I guess I could always ride bareback." Thea didn't sound too enthusiastic, and Lynn didn't blame her. Controlling Oscar was challenging enough when you were safely seated in the saddle. Without a saddle, he had a bad habit of bucking and trying to rid himself of his passenger load as soon as he had a chance.

"That may not be necessary," said David. "I know a guy who has a saddle we can borrow for a few days. One of his horses has a very similar build to Oscar, so I'm pretty sure his saddle should fit. He has no use for it himself at the moment, since his horses are in the pasture for the summer. If you'll wait a minute, I'll go and call him."

Fifteen minutes later, he was back with a saddle which proved to fit perfectly on Oscar's back. Thea was thrilled. Finally, their outing could start.

"Do you want to take the shortcut along the creek?" asked Monica when they got closer to the woods. "The trail isn't very straight there, but you can easily ride on it."

"Great idea!" Thea steered Oscar onto the other trail. Monica, Maria and Lynn followed. It was really nice to ride next to the burbling and rippling sounds of the creek. The horses walked calmly and seemed to enjoy it, too.

Suddenly Maria called out, "SOS! Bag alarm!"

Everyone knew what that meant. Golden Boy's fear of white plastic bags was common knowledge.

Lynn pulled on the reins and used her leg aids to stop Golden Boy, but just then a light gust of wind blew the bag up into the air, and Golden Boy spotted it. At first he just stood there, stiff as a board. Then he jumped to the side and took off straight for the bushes in a total panic. Lynn had her hands full just trying to hold on. He ran through

brush and jumped over rocks, but then, fortunately, Golden Boy ran into a barrier. Two large trees were lying in the road, partially crossed and blocking his escape. For one petrifying moment Lynn thought that Golden Boy would try to jump over the tree trunks, but in the nick of time he changed his mind and came to a sudden stop.

"Ho, ho-o!" said Lynn soothingly. "Don't worry, baby. There's nothing to be afraid of anymore. The scary bag is all gone."

She continued to talk soothingly to Golden Boy, and finally the horse started relaxing. Right afterwards the others arrived, riding between the trees.

"How did it go?" asked Monica. "Are you both okay?"

Lynn nodded. "All good now. Luckily Golden Boy had to stop, whether he wanted to or not."

"Don't you think we should go back to the trail?" Thea asked Lynn. "It should be safe now, since we removed the plastic bag. There were a lot of beer cans and other trash there too, so we're obviously not the only ones who like it in the woods."

As they talked Maria sat on her horse and scouted the area around them. Suddenly she discovered something brown lying under a tree not far away.

"What can that be?" She pointed. "Is it a dead animal?"

"Let's go take a look," said Monica.

Thea arrived at the tree first. She bent down, peered under the branches, and then screamed. "My saddle! Guys, it's my saddle! Somebody's cut it into pieces!"

They all flocked around the saddle. Big slashes crisscrossed the leather. The saddle was completely destroyed.

"How awful!" said Lynn, shocked. "The person who's done this must be sick. Nobody in their right mind would break in and steal a saddle just to destroy it, would they?"

Thea scratched her head. "No, I think you're right. This seems totally insane!"

"Maybe the thief thought it was an expensive saddle that would be worth a lot of money," suggested Maria, half-heartedly. "So when he discovered that it wasn't, he got mad and cut it up in a fit of rage."

"That sounds a little far-fetched to me, but who knows?" Thea shrugged her shoulders. "Either way, the saddle's destroyed..."

A stifled moan came from Monica all of a sudden, and the others looked at her. She was white as a sheet and looked like she might faint at any moment.

"What's the matter, Monica?" said Maria, concerned. "Are you feeling sick?"

"No, it's nothing," mumbled Monica. "Or yes, I don't know..."

She fell silent, unsure whether she ought to say more, but then she blurted it out. "It's just that this reminds me so much of something that happened before. It was these kinds of things Steven did where we lived before. He and his friends would break into people's places, steal things and vandalize. In several places they slashed furniture and

other stuff..."

"Are you saying you think Steven might have done this?" asked Thea shocked.

"No... No! ... I don't know," mumbled Monica, unhappy. "No, I don't really believe that Steven would start doing these kinds of things again. Not now, when everything is going so well! He's got a job and everything, and he no longer has terrible fits of rage the way he used to. But I know Mum's been complaining about him being out half the night lately. He says he's only visiting friends and playing video games and stuff. Of course, there's no way for me to know if that's true or not..."

The group was silent for a while, and then Thea said quietly, "Lynn, didn't your dad say that there have been an unusual number of nighttime burglaries in the area lately?"

"Yes, he did," said Lynn slowly.

"They've stolen stuff worth thousands." She looked at Monica. "Wouldn't you and your mum have noticed if Steven suddenly seemed to have an unusual amount of money?"

"Of course we would! I didn't think about that." Monica looked relieved. "Steven is flat broke right now! He's always broke right before payday, and he definitely doesn't have any more money than usual. It's just me, I'm being silly..."

"I can't imagine Steven would actually be stupid enough to start messing around with criminal activities again," said Maria. "Now that he's finally gotten himself out of that mess. There must be another explanation for the burglaries and what happened to Thea's saddle."

"I'm sure you're right," said Monica quickly, in an attempt to convince herself as well as the rest of them. "Steven wouldn't do something like this now. He knows perfectly well that it would completely crush Mum if he got into trouble with the police again. It must be somebody else. I'm sure of it!"

Monica turned away from the others and started patting Le Bel on the neck. She wanted so desperately to believe a hundred percent that Steven was not involved, but a terrible suspicion crept into her and sat like a stubborn knot in her stomach...

None of them felt like continuing the trip after all that had happened, so they decided to take the mutilated saddle with them and ride back to the stable.

"The police might be interested in seeing it," said Maria, "but how do we take the saddle with us?"

In the end, Monica ended up carrying the saddle in her lap. It was a little cumbersome, but she managed. They rode for a while in silence. Then Lynn said, "I just thought of something. "You know Dad said he's going to keep watch in the stable tonight, right? But it's not at all certain that the thief will come back. He may be satisfied with the damage he's done already, and then we'll never know who it was. Which is why I think we should try to get to the bottom of this!"

"Cool!" said Thea, excited. "I've always wanted to play detective."

"But we don't know anything about investigating," argued Maria. "How are we going to figure out who the thief is? It's not like we can go door to door and ask people, 'Excuse me, sir, but it wasn't you, by any chance, who broke into our stable, was it?'"

"Dummy!" laughed Lynn. "We have to be a lot smarter than that! I –"

"Look!" interrupted Thea, who was riding first.

They had just come out of the woods and were now within view of the ranch.

"The police are here. That's convenient!"

A few minutes later, they were talking to two friendly police officers, about Golden Boy who had been scared by the plastic bag, and about finding the mutilated saddle. But nobody mentioned Steven's name or the fact that Monica had been worried that he might be involved in the vandalism.

"... and we figured you guys might want to see the saddle, so we brought it home with us," finished Maria.

"Hmm! That's too bad. It would have been better to leave it where it was, I'm afraid," said one of the officers. "Then we might have been able to find some useful fingerprints on it."

The girls looked embarrassed as they

exchanged glances. Why hadn't they thought of that? They sure were fine detectives!

After the police left, Lynn said, "Daddy, would it be okay if we let the horses stay in the enclosure while we bike to the supermarket to buy something?"

"Sure. I'll be working in the yard anyway, so I can keep an eye on them. But I think you should go into the kitchen before you go and heat up a pizza or something. If I'm not mistaken, Maria is as hungry as a pack of wolves right now."

David winked at Maria, who looked relieved at the mention of food.

Maria wasn't the only one who was hungry, either. The pizza was gone in no time. They were just finishing eating when Joanna appeared in the doorway. She rubbed her eyes and gave a wide yawn.

"Good morning, girls," she said. "Don't tell me you're having pizza for breakfast!"

"Breakfast?" Lynn rolled her eyes. "Mum, it's after one p.m.!"

"Is it really that late? Oh well, it's no surprise I slept that long. I sat up half the night writing."

"Did you happen to hear anything strange while you were up?" Lynn wanted to know. "Any sound of footsteps or growling or anything?"

"Not a sound. But you know how I am when I'm writing. People could probably shoot off cannons without me noticing. Why do you ask? Did something happen?"

So they had to tell the whole story about the burglary and the mutilated saddle all over again. When they were done, Joanna said, "That's the weirdest thing I've ever heard. I guess I might see one possible explanation, but no... that can't be it. That's not how this happened anyway..."

"What, Mum?" Lynn demanded to know, but her mother wouldn't say any more. She excused herself by saying she needed to think things through properly first.

When they came out in the hallway, David was there, talking on the phone.

"This afternoon?" he said. "It's not the best time for me, but all right, if it's that important, I'll do it."

He ended the conversation and turned to Lynn. "It turns out that I have to go to an important meeting for my company today. My boss, who was supposed to go, has gotten sick all of a sudden. That was he on the phone right now. The bad part is that I won't be able to make it home by tonight."

"But, then who's going to keep watch in the stable?" asked Lynn. She was eagerly anticipating his answer.

"Well...." David hesitated. "I don't really like it, but it seems as if I have no choice but to leave that to you guys. That is, if Thea and Monica's parents also give their consent."

"Of course they will!" the two girls shouted in unison. "Oh, this will be fun!" added Thea.

"But you have to promise me one thing,"

said David as he rummaged through the shelves in the coat closet.

"Ahh! Here it is!" he uttered triumphantly, holding up a small, shiny object. "If you hear anything suspicious tonight, whatever you do, do not go outside to investigate! Instead, you blow as hard as you can on this umpire's whistle. I bet that will make the thief run away as fast as he can."

"You can rely on us, Dad," said Lynn. "We'll scare away any and all burglars that might come by. And I'll take my cell phone too, so I can call Mum if anything happens."

"That's good," said David, but he looked a little worried as he left to go and pack.

Chapter 8
Steven Is Buying a Car

The girls started making plans for their slumber party in the stable as they rode their bikes to the store.

"I assume we should take sleeping bags?" Thea looked questioningly at her friends.

Maria nodded. "Yes, we'll need them. And we should have a bunch of candy and snacks too. It'll be like being on a camping trip, only a lot more exciting!"

"Maria and I will get some goodies at the store, and then we can meet back at our place at 8 p.m.."

"Remember to keep your eyes and ears open while you're at the store," said Thea. "Who knows, you might hear something that will give us a hint about the burglar."

"Our ears will be up like antennas," promised Maria. "Any suggestions on what we should buy? We'll need chocolate, of course, and caramels, potato chips and…"

"Will you stop it? You're a total pig!" sighed Lynn. "I can't understand how somebody who loves candy and junk food as much as you do can be so skinny!"

"Sheer talent," said Maria with a grin.

The kids finally reached the store.

"All right, see you later," said Thea. She and Monica headed off to go home and pack.

When Monica got home, her mother was sitting at the kitchen table drinking a glass of iced tea and reading the newspaper. "Hey, sweetheart, home already? I haven't even started dinner yet. It's so hot, it makes me all sluggish."

"What do you say we drop the cooking and just have some salad or sandwiches later on?" suggested Monica. "Where's Steven, by the way? Wasn't he supposed to get off work early today?"

"Yes, he should be home any minute. How did it go today? Was the horse still wonderful?"

"Totally!" said Monica excited. "Cindy is exactly the kind of horse I've always wanted. She's so nice and gentle, and yet at the same time she has a mischievous twinkle in her eye. Oh, Mum, I wish I was a millionaire! If I was, I would buy her on the spot."

"You would, huh," laughed her mother. Then she got serious. "Oh darling, I wish I could afford to get you a horse for your birthday, but I'm afraid it's just not possible right now."

"I know, Mum, I know." Monica gave her mother a hug. "It's all right. I'll be just fine without a horse. And who knows, maybe I can talk Thomas into letting me ride her a couple times a week if I help him take care of Cindy. But listen, I've got to tell you what happened in the stable last night..."

"Horse talk, horse talk all day, is it?" said a teasing voice suddenly. Monica turned around instantly. Her brother, Steven, was standing in the doorway, grinning from ear to ear.

"I don't know what you'd want an old oat eater like that for," he continued. "Come outside with me, and I'll show you some real horse power!"

Steven disappeared out the door, and Monica and her mother followed, nearly bursting with curiosity. When they got down to the parking lot, Steven threw his hand out toward a dark blue BMW. They could tell it wasn't a new car, but it had just been washed and shined in the sun.

"Well, what do you think?" he asked, looking proud. "Pretty stylish, isn't it?"

"Do you mean to tell me that it's yours?"

"Yup! It's mine, all right. All paid for, cash-and-carry!"

"But... where did you get the money?" his mother asked, shocked. "I hope you didn't take out a bank loan, Steven! You can't afford that on your salary."

"No, I didn't take out a loan, Mum. Don't worry! I just robbed the post office," said Steven with a grin on his face. "Didn't you hear the news today?"

"Verrry funny!" His mother looked sternly at him. "Stop kidding around, and tell me how you got the money!"

"From the football pool, of course," answered Steven. "I've been betting about twenty dollars a week ever since I started my job, and I finally hit bull's-eye. Twelve out of twelve! The jackpot wasn't exactly the biggest we've seen, but it was

enough to buy this old wreck and pay for the insurance."

"Honey, gambling? I don't like to hear that, but… Congratulations, darling. Why didn't you tell me before? You must have known about this for several days," his mother said.

"I wanted to keep it a secret until I'd actually picked up the car. Thought it would be fun to surprise you guys." Steven laughed. "And from the looks on your faces, I think I succeeded. Monica, here, seems speechless. Aren't you going to congratulate me, Sis?"

"Uh... of course!" said Monica bewildered. "This was just so unexpected. Congratulations, Steven!"

She smiled at him, but inside she was crying. Her suspicion sat like a hard knot in her stomach. What if Steven hadn't won the money? What if the money came from those burglaries that Lynn's dad had mentioned? No, of course they didn't! How could she think such a bad thing about her brother? But the bad thoughts continued to haunt her no matter how hard she tried to fight them.

"We should celebrate," said her mother happily. "I'll go inside and find something yummy for us!"

She left, while Monica and Steven stayed by the car.

"Well, well, would you look at that! Did you rob the landfill, Steven?"

Steven turned around instantly. Martin

Olsen was standing next to his beautiful Mercedes, leaning against the door. He snickered condescendingly. "Oh well, I guess some people don't care too much what they drive around in. Personally I wouldn't be caught dead in an old heap like that, but it's probably just fine for a budding criminal like you!"

Steven's face turned white. At first it looked like he wanted to jump on Martin, but instead he turned away and walked into the apartment building without a word.

"That was mean!" Monica stared furiously at Martin. "What has Steven ever done to you to make you treat him like that?"

"Nothing to me personally," said Martin, "but he shoplifted at my dad's store. People like him should be locked up!"

"You're lying! Steven is not a thief!" protested Monica angrily.

She strode purposefully toward the entrance, but once inside she didn't feel nearly as certain as she'd sounded.

When she got back to the apartment, Steven was standing in the kitchen, looking livid. "I'd like to take that conceited brat and cut him into pieces!" he fumed.

"Steven! Don't talk like that!" His mother gave him a shocked look. "I agree that Martin behaved despicably, but saying equally despicable things doesn't help anything!"

"Sorry," mumbled Steven. "I just got so angry. If I'd stayed out there one more second I'd probably have made mincemeat of that little stuck-up wimp!"

"I'm certainly glad you controlled yourself," said Monica. "I don't care much for mincemeat, anyway. And I'm sure Mr. Olsen would have had you arrested in no time if you laid a hand on his precious son."

"Let's just forget about Mr. Olsen and his arrogant son," said their mother firmly. "Let's celebrate Steven's new car instead! What would you like? Ice cream cake or ice cream cake?"

"Ice cream cake sounds good," said Steven, and Monica nodded in agreement.

A few minutes later they were all seated around the kitchen table, each with a big helping of a delicious, chocolate-covered horseshoe-shaped ice cream cake.

"Now, Monica," said her mother. "What were you about to tell me before Steven came in? You said something had happened at the stable. Has there been another burglary attempt?"

"Not just an attempt this time."

Then Monica told the whole story about the break-in and the mutilated saddle. The whole time she was talking, she kept an eye on Steven, to see his reaction. But he didn't seem to have much of a reaction at all. When she had told them everything, he only said lightly, "Sounds pretty lame! Why would anybody bother to steal an ordinary old horse saddle?"

"That's exactly what we're going to find out." Monica gave him a stubborn look. "Which is why Lynn, Thea, Maria and I are going to sleep in the stable tonight. We're going to keep watch in case the thief comes back."

"Sleep in the stable? But couldn't that be dangerous?" objected her mother, concerned.

"No, we'll be fine! Lynn's dad has given us an umpire's whistle, which we'll use if the thief shows up. The mere sound of it will probably scare off the intruder right away. Besides, we'll all have our cell phones and can call Lynn's mum if necessary. Or we can call the police directly. There's no need to worry, Mum. I promise!"

"Well, all right then. If Lynn's parents think it's safe, I guess I don't have any objections," she said. "But promise me you'll be careful!"

"I promise," said Monica.

She glanced over at Steven. He was looking at her with a funny expression on his face. Her suspicion came back in full force. If Steven and the burglar were one and the same person, he would now know that the stable was being watched tonight and would stay away. But was that any proof? They had no guarantee that the thief would come back, regardless of who it was. Ugh, what a mess! Monica shook her head in resignation and went to find her sleeping bag.

She was on her way out of her room when she overheard something that made her stop short. Steven was sitting in the hallway, talking on his cell phone.

"... Yes, I had planned to do it today, but as it turns out, I can't," he said. "I'll have to think about it. I may try to do it tomorrow night, if the coast is clear. Actually, tomorrow will work better regardless, now that I think about it. No, I won't need a horse trailer. Sure, I'll keep you informed!"

Steven hadn't seen her, so Monica withdrew quietly back into her room. So it was true! Steven was involved in something creepy, and now they were evidently planning to steal a horse! She sank down on the bed, on the verge of tears.

Chapter 9
A Night Ride

At eight o'clock the girls gathered again. They were standing in the hallway talking. None of the others noticed that Monica was unusually quiet.

"Do you want to go for a ride before we get the horses ready for the night?" asked Maria. "Since they've been inactive all afternoon, they could probably do with a little exercise."

"Good idea," Lynn concurred. "We can't go to bed yet anyway, and there's nothing good on TV."

They went and picked up the bridles and saddles.

"I talked to my parents," said Thea as she came back carrying the saddle she was borrowing. "They said I can buy a new saddle next week. That'll be nice, even though this one will be fine for a few days."

"Golden Boy!" Lynn called out as they got to the fence surrounding the enclosure. "Come on, boy, I've got a carrot for you."

Golden Boy pointed his ears and then started walking toward Lynn, trailed by Cindy and Le Bel. The only horse who was not coming was Oscar. He stood a few yards away, watching Thea with a mischievous look on his face.

"I guess I'll have to go and get him," sighed Thea. "It's not gonna be easy. I can tell he's in his typical teasing mood."

"I'll help you," offered Lynn. "We'll just tether the others in the meantime."

As expected, Oscar made them work. He bounced and jumped, and escaped cleverly every time they got near him.

"He's driving me crazy!" sighed Thea, annoyed. "Maybe I should start learning lasso throwing, so I can catch him that way."

In the end, Oscar trapped himself, though. He bounced sideways in an elegant arch out of Thea's reach, but failed to notice Maria approaching from the other side.

"Gotcha, you rascal!" she shouted victoriously as she grabbed hold of his bridle. Oscar knew the game was over, and came willingly with Maria out to the other horses.

As they were getting ready Thea asked, "So where should we go? We can't go too far, since it's getting kind of late."

"Let's ride up to the small abandoned farm," suggested Lynn. "That's a nice little

trip that won't take more than an hour or so."

They let the horses walk on loose reins. All four of the horses were well fed and lazy and seemed perfectly happy to walk leisurely at their own pace. Half an hour later, they got to the small, dilapidated farm. A blue VW Golf was parked in the farmyard.

"Gee!" exclaimed Thea. "There are people here. Who would want to rent an old shack like this? I can't believe they managed to get the car all the way up here, either. The road is really bumpy and full of potholes! By the way, isn't that the same car we saw in the woods the other day?"

She looked quizzically at the others.

"Yes, I think it is. At least it looks exactly like it," said Maria, and Lynn nodded.

Monica didn't say anything.

Suddenly they noticed that the curtain behind one of the dirty windows moved slightly. Evidently, somebody inside was watching them.

"I don't like this!" uttered Lynn. "Let's go back!"

They turned the horses around and rode back home, at a greater speed than the trip out.

"What if it's the burglar, bunking up there?" said Thea excitedly, when they got closer to the stable. "Maybe we just stumbled on his hiding place."

"I wish you were right," uttered Monica suddenly in a low voice, "but I'm afraid I already know who the thief is. It's Steven!"

She collapsed on Cindy's back, lying forward with her head in the horse's neck as she started sobbing. Cindy gave a start at first, but stayed calm.

Monica cried and cried. The others pulled her down from Cindy's back and tried their best to comfort her. Finally the sobbing subsided into wounded gasps.

"Why are you so sure that it's your brother?" asked Maria softly.

So Monica told them the whole story about Steven and his supposed winnings, and about the phone conversation that she had overheard. When she was finished, the group was quiet for a long time.

Then Maria said, "It kind of sounds like

Steven had planned to come here tonight and take one of the horses, but when he learned that we'll be keeping watch on the stable he postponed it and plans to break in tomorrow night instead! But how can he be so sure that we won't be keeping watch then, too?"

"I have no idea. Do you think I should go home and tell my mum about it? Or should I let Steven know that he's been found out? I don't really want to do either."

Lynn shook her head. "No, I think we should wait until tomorrow before we say anything at all. If you go home now and accuse Steven of being a horse thief, he'll just deny it. Besides, there's always the possibility that Steven is actually innocent, and that the phone conversation you overheard had another perfectly natural explanation."

"I agree with Lynn," said Maria. "Let's just sleep in the stable tonight as planned. If the thief is someone else, other than Steven, he may come tonight, and then we'll catch him red-handed! And if not, we'll keep watch tomorrow night too, and see what happens!"

Thea looked at Monica. "I'll understand perfectly if you decide you'd rather go home and sleep there. It can't be much fun for you to sit here and wait to see if your brother is going to break into the stable, tonight or tomorrow."

"No, I'm staying," Monica said very firmly. "It would be a lot worse to be at home and not have any idea what's going on."

"All right, then it's settled," said Lynn with a nod. "C'mon, let's hurry up and go home so we can get the horses ready for the night and have some supper."

Chapter 10
Nighttime in the Stable

It was four rather preoccupied girls who, a short time later, stood in the stable and groomed their horses. Oscar was upset at Thea for not paying enough attention to him, so he nipped her in the arm.

"Ouch!" cried Thea in surprise, and hit him with the brush. "Shame on you, Oscar! Don't you dare do that again, do you hear me?"

Oscar actually did look a little ashamed, but not for long. Shortly after, he started stomping his hind legs and neighing, as if he was saying, "Can you be done with this now, so that a poor horse can get some sleep?"

Thea had to laugh. "Don't be so impatient," she whispered in his ear. "If you're a good boy and stand still, I'll give you a carrot."

At the mention of "carrot" Oscar pointed his ears, and he actually stood still until Thea was done.

When the horses had been fed and gotten their treats, Lynn said, "Do you want to clean the bridles and saddles now, or should we wait until after we've eaten?"

The always-hungry Maria said quickly, "Let's eat first!"

Lynn laughed out loud. "Spoken by an empty stomach! As a matter of fact, it wouldn't exactly hurt the saddles if we let

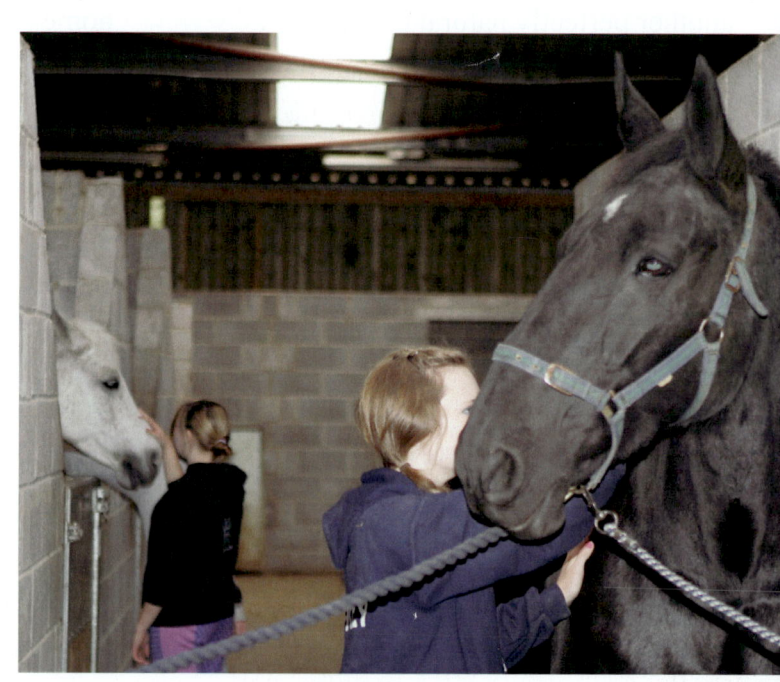

them wait until tomorrow for once. Come on, let's go and raid the fridge."

When they got inside, Joanna was sitting by her computer, drinking tea and reading her notes. Rufus lay across her legs, napping, but when the girls walked in he instantly jumped up and started wagging his tail.

"Hey, Mum! Is there anything good to eat in the fridge?" asked Lynn.

Joanna lifted her head with a totally absent-minded look. "The body is in the freezer, not in the fridge!"

Monica, Thea and Maria stared at her in complete shock.

"Mother!" Lynn rolled her eyes. "Snap out of it, will you? I was asking about food!"

"Oh! Of course," said Joanna, patting

her own cheek. "You'll have to forgive me, girls. I was completely absorbed by my novel, in which somebody has just found a body in the freezer. But the food – yes, that's in the fridge. We've got a bunch of good stuff for sandwiches, and there's fresh bread in the bread box."

After they had eaten and been in the bathroom to get ready for bed, they said goodnight to Joanna.

"You'd better take Rufus with you," she suggested. "I'll feel a little better if he's out there too, even though he proved to be a lousy guard dog last night."

"Yeah, actually, I'm still wondering why he didn't bark last night," commented Lynn. "It's all right if he comes with us. If you hear the whistle you'll call the police, right?"

"You can be sure of it! Or you can call me on your cell phone. I'll carry the phone with me, so I'll be sure to hear it if you call."

The horses looked surprised to see the girls when they returned to the stable. They weren't used to visitors so late at night.

Monica went over to Cindy and started scratching her mane. "Good night, Cindy," she said quietly. "We'll make sure that no bad guys come and disturb you and your friends tonight."

Cindy snorted contentedly. She obviously liked being fussed over.

Maria, who was standing by Le Bel and stroking his muzzle, asked, "Where do you guys want to sleep, by the way? In one of the empty stalls?"

Lynn nodded. "Yeah, we can just spread a bunch of straw on the floor and roll out our sleeping bags on top of it. We may not have a lot of elbow room, but it'll be cozy."

They got the straw, and then picked up their sleeping bags. It was clear that at least Rufus thought this was a lot of fun. He scampered back and forth inside the stall, and got in the way everywhere he went. Finally Lynn had to hold him so the others could get everything in place. Then they crawled into their sleeping bags. It was quiet for a while, and then Maria said, "Anybody want some chocolate? I've got an assortment here."

"Woof!" said Rufus, jumping toward her. He took a shortcut over Lynn's stomach.

"Rufus, you're such a brute," scolded Lynn. "You can't just walk all over me like that!"

But Rufus couldn't care less. Surely, Lynn didn't expect him to take all kinds of long detours when there was a yummy treat being offered! Maria, who knew that chocolate is bad for dogs, fished out a couple of other treats which she gave him, and watched him wolf them down in a flash. When he realized that she wasn't going to give him anymore, he padded back to his corner of the stall and lay down. The girls stayed awake for a while, chatting and eating chocolate. Then Lynn said, "We should probably turn out the lights now, to make the stable look normal."

"I'll get the light," said Thea, who was

closest to the switch. "Maybe we ought to be quiet too, so we can't be heard from the outside."

It didn't take long before Thea and Maria were both asleep. Minutes ticked away and turned into hours.

Monica was still wide-awake, but Lynn was on the verge of falling asleep when Rufus suddenly stirred. He got up, walked over to the door and started growling in a low voice.

"The burglar!" Lynn whispered excited. "Where's the whistle?" She rummaged desperately through the straw. "Oh good, here it is!" Lynn stood up quietly and tiptoed gently toward the door. Just then, Rufus stopped growling. Instead he started whining and wagging his tail!

"Mum?" Lynn called out. "Is that you?"

But no sound could be heard from the outside, and shortly after Rufus stopped whining and went back to the stall. Lynn followed him. Thea and Maria had woken up from the noise, and Maria asked quietly, "What's going on? Is somebody outside?"

"I don't know." Lynn shrugged her shoulders. "Rufus started growling at first, but then he stopped and started wagging his

tail instead. It was probably nothing, or maybe he got the whiff of an animal or something. I didn't hear anything suspicious, at least."

"Hush! What was that?" said Monica all of a sudden.

They sat quietly and listened, and now they could all hear it.

"A car," whispered Thea. "Probably just some car driving by on the road."

The sound grew fainter as the car drove away, and after a while they couldn't hear it anymore.

Chapter 11
Detectives United, Inc.

Nothing more happened that night, but even though everything was quiet the girls couldn't go back to sleep. Not until dawn did they start dozing off, and none of them slept very soundly. Hence, it was a pretty sleepy gang who walked slowly up to the house around seven a.m. to have some breakfast. The only one who looked awake and alert was Rufus.

Joanna was not up yet, so they tried to be as quiet as possible in order to not wake her. Just as they had finished eating, she walked into the kitchen, yawning.

"I thought I heard voices," she said. "Good morning."

She looked at them more closely. "Gee! Did you guys stay up all night? You don't look like you've slept much."

"We didn't," answered Lynn, "even though not much happened. That is, Rufus growled once, but then he started wagging his tail, so it must not have been anything. And afterwards we heard a car on the road, but it drove away."

"So nobody tried to get into the stable during the night?"

"No, because he knew we were going to be there," stated Monica in a low voice. It looked as if she was on the verge of tears again.

Joanna gave her a confused glance.

"It's a long story," said Lynn reluctantly.

"Well, I'd like to hear it anyway." Joanna sat down at the table. "I'll come down to the stable after I've eaten and changed my clothes."

"Okay," said Lynn. "We'll take care of the horses now."

They had just gotten their grooming boxes out when they heard a car outside. Shortly after, Martin appeared in the stable doorway.

"Hi there!" he said. "My, what a bunch of busy beavers you are so early in the morning."

Nobody answered. Monica turned her back to him. She hadn't forgotten what he said to Steven the day before. The only one who greeted him in a friendly manner was Rufus. The dog scuttled about around Martin's legs, wagging his tail and turning on the charm.

"Rufus, come here!" Lynn gave the dog a stern look.

"Ouch! Apparently, I'm not very popular around here, am I?" Martin winked at Lynn. She blushed and didn't know what to answer to that.

"Actually, I just came to ask if you have an available stall," he continued, "'cause I assume you're not gonna keep sleeping in the stable every night? The thing is, my sister is coming home from Paris for the summer, and she's thinking of leasing a horse and brushing up on her riding skills while she's here. So she asked me to find an available stall for her at a boarding stable, and naturally I immediately thought of this one!"

"You'll have to talk to my dad about that," said Lynn dismissively. "He's the one who deals with the boarding leases and such. He's not home at the moment, but he should be back before noon. You can call him if you want."

"All right." Martin smiled. "I'll do that."

The girls stood in the doorway and watched him while he got into his car and started the engine. Suddenly he rolled down the window and called out to Monica.

"Tell your brother he needs to get a muffler for that heap of junk he's driving. When he drove by our house late last night, it sounded like World War III was breaking out!"

"Was Steven out driving last night?" Monica stared at him. "How do you know it was him? He's not the only one who has a car around here."

"I had just gotten out of bed because I was thirsty. And I happened to be standing in the kitchen drinking some water when his car thundered by. I think it was two thirty or something like that. You may want to tell your mother to keep a better eye on her son," said Martin arrogantly. Then he stepped on the gas pedal and drove down the driveway in a cloud of dust.

"What an obnoxious guy!" exclaimed Lynn. "If he was the one who was leasing a horse and wanted a stall, I'd say no way! But his sister is actually pretty nice, and..."

She was interrupted by Maria, who suddenly shouted, "Of course! "How stupid of me! Why didn't I think of that before? Lynn, I've got to talk to your mother. I think I know what she meant when she..."

The rest of her sentence was left hanging in the air as Maria whirled around and stormed up to the house. The others just

stood there, staring after her with dumbfounded looks on their faces.

"What in the world's gotten into her?" exclaimed Thea finally. "Did she get heatstroke or something?"

"You've got me." Lynn shrugged her shoulders. "I guess we'll find out when she comes back. In the meantime, we'd better take care of these poor, starving horses."

As if on cue, Oscar started neighing a loud complaint.

"Take it easy, boy, I'm coming!" shouted Thea. "You're the biggest fusser of the whole bunch, do you know that?"

Thea hurried into the feed room and picked up a piece of carrot for her horse. He munched it down greedily and then tilted his head and begged for more.

"Oh, no!" laughed Thea. "I don't feel that sorry for you. You got a treat already, and that's enough. Now you can eat your hay while I make you all nice and shiny."

Lynn had already started brushing Golden Boy.

"If Maria doesn't get back before we're done with our own horses, I guess we should brush Le Bel too," she suggested.

"I'm sure she'll be back long before we're done," commented Thea.

Monica didn't say anything. She made a half-hearted attempt at brushing Cindy, but it seemed she couldn't muster up much strength for anything. With a sigh she sat down on the straw inside Cindy's stall. As she sat, she thought about Steven and how

difficult life had suddenly become. Now, when everything could have been so nice! She gave another sigh, this time so heavily that Cindy turned her head and looked at her with surprise. That made Monica smile, despite her sadness.

"Oh Cindy, you're the cutest thing in the world!" She stroked the horse lovingly on the muzzle. Cindy looked at Monica with her big, gentle eyes. Then she nudged her while letting out a low snort. Monica patted the mare's neck, ruffled her mane, and then finally got to her feet and continued grooming.

"There," said Thea a little later. "I'm done with this rascal!"

"I'm just gonna pick out Golden Boy's hooves, then I'll be done too." Lynn glanced toward the door. "I wonder what Maria's up to? She's been gone forever!"

No sooner had she said it than Maria came running, her cheeks flushed and her eyes gleaming with excitement.

"Would you guys mind terribly if I asked you to brush Le Bel for me?" she asked. "Joanna and I have to go to the police station really quick. We'll be back soon!"

Before the others had a chance to ask a single question, she was gone. Lynn ran out just in time to see her mother's car heading down the driveway. Shaking her head, she went back into the stable and started taking care of Le Bel.

When all the ponies were fed and groomed, and they had mucked out all the stalls, the girls sat down outside the stable and waited for Maria and Joanna to come back from their mysterious expedition. They waited a long time before they finally heard the sound of an approaching car.

"It's about time!" Thea exclaimed. "I'm dying to find out what's going on!"

"Same here!" Lynn got up eagerly. Then she let out a sigh of disappointment. It wasn't her mother's station wagon that was coming after all, it was a taxi. The cab stopped in the farmyard and David stepped out. He barely had time to pay the driver before his daughter practically assaulted him.

"Daddy, I'm so glad you came," she shouted. "Mum and Maria are at the police station… they were super mysterious and odd, and wouldn't tell us anything before

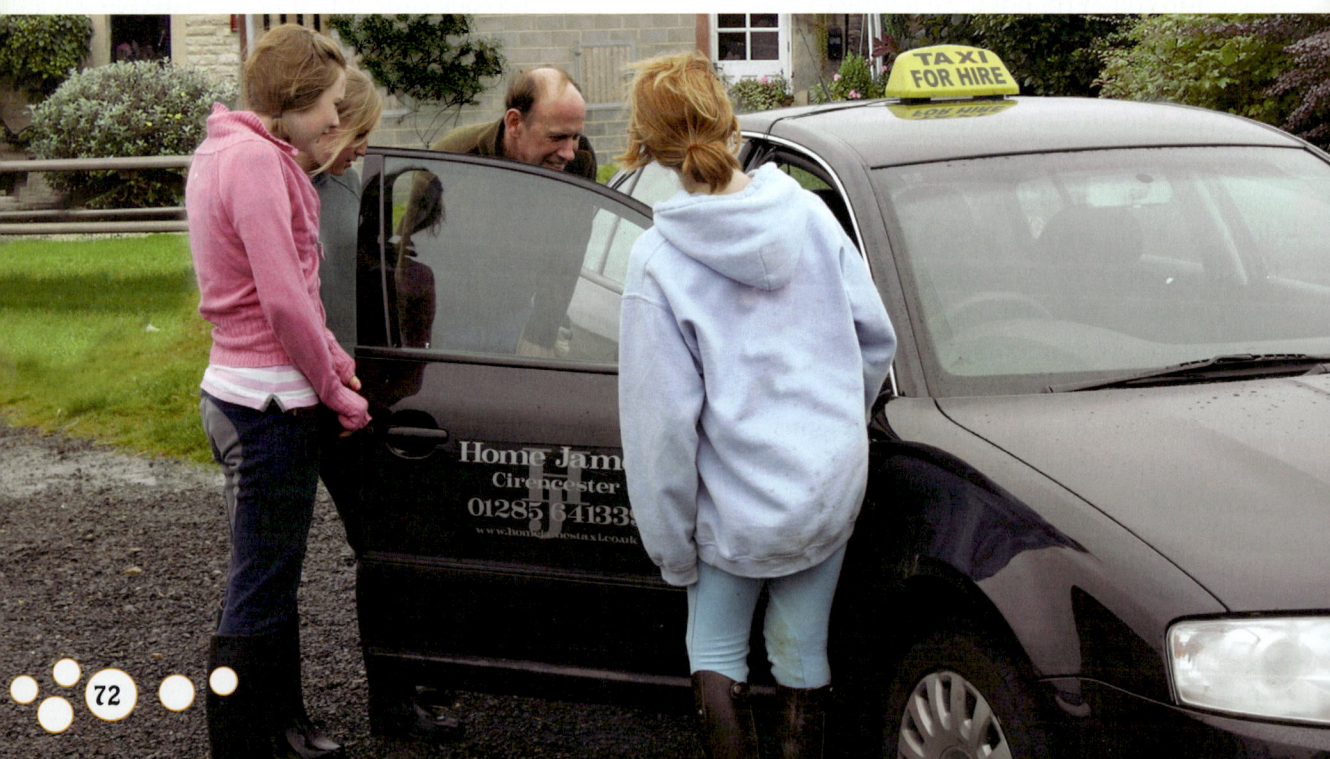

they left, and now they've been gone for an eternity and I –"

"Hey, hey, slow down!" David raised her hands in defense. "I have no idea what you're talking about. Have Joanna and Maria turned themselves in to the police because they're behaving strangely?"

"Daddy!" Lynn groaned. "Sit down and I'll tell it to you s-l-o-w-l-y, so that you can u-n-d-e-r-s-t-a-n-d it."

"Impertinent girl!" David pinched Lynn's behind. "What did I do to deserve such a daughter?"

"Nothing, you were just really lucky!" Lynn giggled and jumped away to a safe distance in case her dad continued to play lobster.

They sat down under the large tree in the farmyard. After David heard the whole story about Maria's strange behavior, he shook his head and said, "I don't understand it any more than you do. We'll just have to wait until they get back, I guess."

For a while nobody said anything, then Lynn suddenly remembered something. "Oh! I was supposed to tell you. Martin Olsen was here this morning and asked about leasing a stall. His sister is coming home from Paris, and she wants to ride this summer."

"I see," said David. "I guess we could arrange that. We do have an available stall. Soon to be two, in fact."

"Two?" Lynn gave him a surprised look. "Is one of the race horses moving? Or do you mean Le Bel's stall, after Maria has gone home at the end of the summer?"

"No, actually I meant Cindy's stall," said her dad. "I was just over at the supermarket on my way home, and while I was there I ran into Thea and Thomas's mother. She told me that Thomas has sold Cindy."

"What?" Thea gasped. "Thomas sold Cindy? To whom?"

"That I don't know. Thomas just called home this morning and told her that the horse was sold. I guess the buyer might be somebody at the place where he's staying on his camping trip."

Monica suddenly felt a big lump in her throat. It kept getting bigger, and she got worried that she would start bawling right in front of everybody. How stupid she had been! Here she was, conjuring up some rosy red dream about sharing the responsibility of Cindy's care with Thomas. She should have known that he was going to sell the horse. After all, he had told them straight out that he wasn't interested in horses anymore.

Before Monica could stop, her eyes welled up and two big tears trickled down her cheeks. She jumped up and turned away from the others.

"I'm just going to the bathroom," she said in a stifled voice before she ran toward the house.

Lynn and Thea both understood what had happened.

"Poor Monica," sighed Lynn sympathetically. "She was probably hoping that she could ride Cindy sometimes after Thomas got back."

"It wasn't very nice of him to sell the

horse without letting us know," said Thea. She was angry. "How does he know that Cindy will have a good home when he's selling her to some stranger who lives that far away?"

"I'm sure..." started David, but suddenly fell silent, looking out toward the road. "About time," he mumbled and got up.

The family car turned into the farmyard, stopped, and Maria and Joanna jumped out. They looked extremely pleased with themselves.

"Hi there!" said Joanna with a smile.

"Here we are. Should we go inside and make some lunch? I'm starving."

"Don't you dare keep us waiting any longer!" Lynn was so impatient she could hardly stand still. "What did you talk to the police about? And what –?"

"Sorry! Our lips are zipped and sealed!" replied Joanna, being theatrical. "You'll have to wait, I'm afraid. But soon there shall be a big finale, when Detectives United, Inc. will reveal all and the truth shall be known to the worrrrrld!"

"Good grief, Mum, you sound like a very bad play!" exclaimed Lynn annoyed.

"C'mon, out with it!"

"I'm sorry, I can't!" Joanna finally got serious. "The police have forbidden us to say anything. In fact, we had to promise not to breathe a word until the whole thing is over, so, Maria and I can't tell you anything until tomorrow morning."

"Tomorrow morning?" David looked confused. "How do you know the whole thing will be resolved by morning?"

"Because Maria and I are going to see to it that it is!" Joanna flung her arms out delightedly. "And you guys will help us."

"How can we help you when we don't even know what's going on?" asked Lynn irritably.

"You'll just have to do as you're told," said her mother.

While they were talking, Monica had come out of the house. Her eyes were red, but she looked calm and collected.

"What exactly do you want us to do?" she asked quietly.

"You have to go camping!"

Chapter 12
Found Out

Everyone except Maria stared at Joanna in disbelief. Had she completely lost it?

"Let me get this straight," said David. "Did you say we're going camping?"

"Not you." Joanna laughed. "Lynn, Maria, Thea and Monica will sleep in a tent in the woods tonight. That is, if Thea and Monica get permission from their parents, of course."

"Oh, I'm sure I can go," said Thea, excited.

Monica nodded. "Me too, as long as I'm home tomorrow afternoon. It's my birthday tomorrow, and my mother always makes something extra special for the occasion."

"If everything goes according to plan, the mystery should be solved by the time you come back from the woods tomorrow morning," Joanna said.

"Who's going to look after the horses while we're gone?" Lynn wanted to know. "You and Daddy?"

"Nope. We're going on a visit to Uncle Oliver and Aunt Randi's tonight," said her mother. "We'll take Rufus with us too, and won't be back until late night."

"But... if we all go away, the burglar will be free to do as he pleases!" Thea stared at Lynn's mother in confusion.

"Exactly!" said Joanna victoriously.

Four pair of eyes stared incomprehensibly at her. Now they were sure she must have lost it.

Maria couldn't help laughing at the looks of their faces. "I think you'll have to tell them a little more," she said to Joanna.

"Yeah, I guess you're right, otherwise they might just walk around with blank stares for the rest of their lives." Joanna turned toward the others. "You see, the whole point is to make the burglar know that the coast is clear. Then he'll come and try to get whatever it is he's been after all along. What he won't know is that the police will be hiding out in the stable!"

"That's brilliant!" Thea looked at her with admiration. "But what made the police suddenly gain an interest in this? Earlier they didn't even want to listen to us!"

"That part you'll find out tomorrow morning." Joanna gave her a mysterious smile. "Now, let's go inside and have some lunch. Oh, and you'd better lock the stable door, so the thief won't just walk in and take off with his loot while we're sitting in the kitchen discussing how we're going to outsmart him!"

The food went down in a flash. After they were finished eating and had cleared the table, Joanna suggested that they put the horses in the pasture.

"David and I will sit outside in the farmyard and keep an eye on both them and the stable," she said.

"But we want to go for a ride," Monica commented hesitantly.

"I'm afraid that will have to wait until the thief has been caught." Joanna's voice was firm. "You guys have had a lot of luck so far. I get goose bumps thinking about the times you've been riding around in the woods lately!"

"But if it's so dangerous in the woods, then why are you telling us to go there to sleep in a tent tonight?" asked Thea puzzled.

"It's not dangerous as long as you don't have the horses with you."

Joanna thought for a moment, and then she continued, "I have a job for you. I'd like you to go to the store and buy a few things for your little adventure. And while you're there, I want you to make a point of talking about spending the night in the woods tonight. Make sure you speak loud and clear. Tell anyone who cares to listen, and remember to also mention that David and I are taking Rufus and going out of town tonight too. If you're lucky, Mrs. Peterson will be at the cash register. She's better than any news agency. Anyone interested in knowing that the stable will be unguarded tonight should hear about it in no time at all."

"As you wish! We'll spread the word," said Thea, making a military hand salute.

The girls took the horses out to the pasture. They horses didn't mind one bit about having a chance to graze in the meadow. Oscar was so excited that he started heading toward the green enclosure immediately. Thea clamped on to his lead rope and tried to hold him back, but ended up being pulled along behind him. Oscar stopped at the gate just long enough for her to unhook the lead rope from the carabiner on his halter. As soon as he realized he was free, he danced off into the meadow and started munching on the bright green grass greedily.

Thea had to laugh. "I just hope he doesn't overeat and get colic! He's so greedy, it's almost scary."

"Don't worry," said Maria. "We won't be gone for more than an hour or two. He was in the pasture longer than that the other day, without a problem. If you're worried that he might eat until he collapses, you can always put him inside when we get back from the store."

They got their bikes and rode to the supermarket to spread the word about their camping trip. They were happy to notice that Mrs. Peterson really was at the cash register. She was a very friendly lady, who loved to chat with everybody. They figured their little news story was guaranteed to get around.

Afterwards, Thea and Monica went home to ask for permission to go camping in the woods while Maria and Lynn stayed outside the store in hopes of seeing people they knew so they could mention the story. Half an hour later, the four of them were together again.

"We both got permission to go," said Monica. She looked pale and unhappy. "Steven was home too. We needn't have bothered to spread the news to others. You should have seen him when I told him about our camping trip. He looked delighted and mumbled something about how convenient it was. I was almost tempted to warn him, but then I thought that if he gets away with it this time, he might keep doing worse things later. So I kept quiet, even though it wasn't easy!"

"I can easily imagine how hard this must be for you!" Thea's voice was filled with sympathy.

The girls didn't say much as they biked back to the farm. They were all preoccupied by their own thoughts. After they had picked up the horses in the pasture and put them inside the stable, they gathered up tent equipment, sleeping bags and food.

"Just toss everything in the back of the truck," said David. "I'll drive you guys as far as the old lumber road goes."

"Will you feed the horses tonight before you go out of town?" asked Lynn.

"Yes, of course. I assume they don't need any oats or pellets tonight, since none of them were ridden today?"

Maria shook her head. "No, they just need a hay net each."

When they reached the clearing in the woods, David turned off the engine. "Do you need any help setting up the tent?" he asked as he unloaded the stuff.

"Nope. We know how to do it," answered Thea confidently. "Besides, we need something to do, so the evening doesn't seem too long."

David drove back to the farm and the girls were left in the woods by themselves.

As they struggled to put the tent up, Thea said, "You know what? I don't feel at all like staying here tonight. We'll miss all the action!"

"Me neither." Lynn looked at the others. "I suggest that we wait until dusk, and then we sneak back to the farm."

"I like that idea!" Thea clapped her hands excitedly. "What about the rest of you? What do you think?"

"I'm not sure about this," said Maria slowly. "I've kind of promised to lie low. And what if the thief sees us and runs away before the police have a chance to catch him?"

"Nobody is going to see me, at least!" said Thea firmly. "I intend to sneak through the woods, as quiet as a ghost!"

"Oohoo! Thea, the invisible lady has spoken!" joked Lynn in a theatrical voice,

and they all burst out laughing. That is, all except Monica. She didn't laugh.

"I think I'll stay here and look after the tent while you guys go and play your little spying game," she said. "I couldn't bear to watch while the police catch Steven and arrest him. He is my brother, after all, and I love him, no matter what he's done!"

"I understand. Of course you don't have to go." Thea put her arm around Monica's shoulder and gave her a quick hug. "Won't you be afraid to stay here all by yourself, though?"

Monica shook her head.

But Maria looked worried. "I don't like the thought of leaving you here all by yourself," she said. "Besides, I think you might regret it if you don't come."

She got another declining headshake from Monica.

"Please!" Maria tried her best to convince her. "Please come with us. I'm sure it won't be as bad as you think, and..."

"I don't want to, okay?!" interrupted Monica stubbornly.

"All right then, I can't force you." Maria shrugged her shoulders helplessly. After that they didn't talk any more about the issue.

At ten o'clock the others said goodbye to Monica and started walking toward the farm. They spoke in whispers to each other at first, but as they got closer to the edge of the woods they stopped talking and focused on being as silent as possible. Lynn pointed toward some underbrush at the edge of the woods. From there, they would have an open view straight toward the stable. They ducked behind the bushes and sat down to wait. All of them were in agony with suspense.

"I don't see any sign of people anywhere," whispered Thea after a while. "What if the police aren't there? What if the stable isn't being watched at all?"

"Of course they're there!" Maria looked at her with irritation. "They're just hiding. That's the whole point, for the stable to look deserted!"

"Hush!" hissed Lynn. "Did you hear that?"

Then they all heard it. The sound of a car! It sounded like the car was approaching from somewhere inside the woods, and it was getting louder all the time. Then all of a sudden it got quiet, but not for long. They heard a car door shut, and then they heard a muted rustle and approaching footsteps.

The three girls hiding in the underbrush held their breaths in suspense. All of a sudden a dark figure slid past them only a few yards away and continued toward the stable. Was it Steven? thought Lynn, sending a thought of sympathy to Monica.

When the figure in the dark clothes reached the stable door, another figure also appeared. At first Lynn thought it was a policeman who had been hiding behind the stable, but then she realized that the two were talking quietly and it became clear that they knew each other.

Shortly after, they heard a series of scraping and banging noises, followed by a long creaking noise. They were breaking open the stable door. The two men went inside the stable and the girls waited in suspense. They didn't have to wait long. Suddenly there was a lot of noise inside the stable, and a dark figure came storming outside. He ran straight for the bushes where the girls were hiding. A police officer came running after him, but the runaway was faster, having gotten a head start.

"He's getting away! We've got to do something!" hissed Thea, and before any of the others could react, she jumped out from her hiding place and blocked the trail in front of the man. The scream she let out was loud enough to scare anyone. The burglar jumped aside in shock, but stumbled on something and fell headfirst to the ground. Seconds later, a breathless police

officer handcuffed him and pulled him to his feet. At this point Maria and Lynn also came out from behind the bushes.

"Gee!" exclaimed the police officer. "A bush full of girls! What the heck are you girls doing out here in the middle of the night?"

"My parents own this farm," answered Lynn. "We knew that the burglar might be coming tonight so we were hiding here in order to keep an eye on the stable. We had no idea there would be two thieves!"

"Have you seen this guy before?" asked the policeman.

The girls shook their heads. The man, who appeared to be in his twenties, was a complete stranger to them.

"Why were you breaking into our stable?" Lynn asked him angrily.

The prisoner only stared at her with a surly face. "Ik begrijp niet," he finally said.

"What?" Lynn looked at him in surprise. "Is he German?"

"Not German. Dutch," said Maria.

"Come back to the stable with me," said the policeman, "and I'll introduce you to his friend. I'm sure you'll know him."

The police officer took a firm grip of the prisoner's arm and then they all walked down to the stable. Just as they turned into the farmyard, three people showed up in the stable doorway. The first one was a police officer, and he was carrying a saddle.

"That's my saddle!" said Maria quickly to Thea. "That's the one the thieves have been after all along!"

Then came another police officer, with a firm grip around the arm of...

"Martin?" gasped Lynn. "Why in the world would he be committing a crime? His dad gives him everything he wants!"

Martin, who kept silent and lowered his eyes, looked as if he wished the ground would swallow him up. His cocky manners were gone.

One of the police officers fished out a walkie-talkie and sent a brief message. Shortly after, a police car appeared in the driveway. The prisoners were placed in the back seat, and then the car drove away.

The three girls stood and watched it leave. Then Lynn shook her head, turned around and walked right into... Steven!

Chapter 13

Birthday Party in the Middle of the Night

Monica sat up in her sleeping bag inside the tent thinking, weren't they going to come back soon? It felt like an eternity since they left. She was beginning to regret that she hadn't gone with them. She would have never guessed just how dark and scary a night in the woods could be, and how many creepy sounds there were! Songwriters who write music about the wonderful peace of the forest have obviously never spent a night there. It seemed like hundreds of tiny, invisible creatures were everywhere, padding around in the dark, sounding like they were headed right toward her and the tent. Anything – even watching Steven be arrested – would have been better than sitting there, all alone inside a skimpy, thin tent, which was no protection against anything, except maybe a rain shower. What if there were wild, dangerous animals outside? What if...

Finally, somebody was coming. She checked the time. It was 12:45 a.m.. She crept as quietly as she could over to the tent opening and peered outside. To her great relief, she recognized Thea. Suddenly the night was not as dark and scary anymore.

But why was Thea alone? Where were the others?

"Monica, come with me! You have no idea what exciting things that have happened!" panted Thea when she got to the tent. "Hurry! Maria was right! You should have come with us..."

She grabbed Monica's hand and pulled her up.

"Hey! Wait, let me get some shoes on first!" protested Monica. "What happened? Why do I have to go? Is it Steven? Was he hurt when the police took him?"

"No, no! Steven isn't hurt, and he isn't arrested either! They did, however, arrest Martin Olsen and some creepy Dutch guy. C'mon now! I'm not saying another word! You'll have to wait until we get to the farm."

And with that, Thea ran off again, and Monica had no choice but to follow her. She was totally confused. Martin had been arrested? Did that mean that Steven was innocent? That seemed too good to be true!

When they arrived, breathless, in the farmyard, Monica was surprised to discover that several cars were parked there. Lynn's parents had apparently come home, and she also saw Thea's parents' car – and Steven's blue BMW! What was going on? Thea flung open the front door and hurried inside. Monica followed her hesitantly.

"This way!" Thea pushed the door to the living room wide open. "David has everyone gathered for a combined meeting... and a birthday party!"

Monica stopped in the doorway, and her mouth fell open.

"Happy Birthday!" shouted a chorus of voices.

"What... who... how...?" stuttered Monica. She thought she must be dreaming. Inside the living room the table was set with party stuff, and her mother was there, and Steven, and everyone were smiling at her.

Thea's parents, Lynn's mother, Maria and Lynn. They were all there. Then Lynn's dad came in from the kitchen, carrying a steaming hot pizza.

"Come in and sit down, Monica," he said with a friendly smile. "You look like you've fallen out of the sky."

"No, just out of a tent..." answered Monica, bewildered, and they all laughed.

"Well, I'm sure you and some of the others here are wondering what's been going on around here lately," said David next. "I'll let Maria explain, since she was the one who first unraveled the mystery."

They all looked expectantly at Maria.

"Well, the whole thing actually started back during Easter break, when Lynn visited me in the Netherlands," said Maria. "One

day, while we were in Amsterdam, we ran into Martin Olsen. He offered to drive us home. And even though he doesn't have the slightest interest in horses, he started showing an unusual interest when he heard that I was planning to come here for my summer vacation and that I was going to take Le Bel with me. At some point he even had me describe Le Bel's saddle in detail for him."

"Yeah, I remember I thought it was kind of funny that he was suddenly so interested," Lynn added.

"As most of you know, there was a break-in at our stable a few days before I came here," continued Maria. "Nothing was stolen, but what we didn't know was that Le Bel's saddle had been removed and replaced with one that looked exactly the same."

"At least on the outside," added David. "The stuffing inside, on the other hand, was a bit different... It consisted of a bunch of small bags, see. In those bags were drugs, worth a million dollars!"

"A million dollars?" Monica gasped. "No wonder the thieves were desperate to get it back!"

"They probably figured this would be as easy as pie," said Maria. "Who would suspect a 14-year-old horse-crazy girl like me of smuggling drugs into the country? Their plan was to remove the saddle containing the drugs and replace it with my own saddle as soon as I got to the farm."

"Martin's friend sent Maria's saddle from Amsterdam by overnight delivery," said David. "He thought it might look too suspicious to be driving around with a horse saddle in the car."

"Why?" Lynn looked questioningly at her dad. "I mean, if anyone asked, he could have just said it was a gift for his cousin, or something like that."

"Well, evidently he didn't think of that. Criminals aren't always the most intelligent people around, you know." David shrugged his shoulders. "Anyway, he sent the package, but something went wrong during transit, and the saddle disappeared."

"Maybe it ended up at a post office in Central Mongolia instead of here," suggested Maria with a giggle.

"Oh, I get it!" Thea exclaimed. "So instead of secretly switching it, they had to actually steal the saddle."

Maria nodded. "That's right. But they had some rotten luck. The first time they tried, Rufus interfered by barking and waking up everybody, and the second time they ended up with the wrong saddle, because they took yours. I would have liked to have sees their faces when they opened the saddle and discovered there were no drugs!"

"You'd better be glad you were nowhere near them at the time!" Steven gave her a serious look. "Drug traders aren't playing."

Lynn shuddered. "So there was actually somebody spying on us in the woods, then! It was probably Martin or his friend sneaking around, waiting for an opportunity to take the saddle."

"That's right," said Maria. "The two of them were taking turns keeping an eye on us, in case a golden opportunity opened up. Then they wouldn't need to break in again. Do you remember when Rufus disappeared that day we were at the lake?"

The others nodded.

"No wonder he seemed full and tired when he got back. Martin had given him a bunch of food and made friends with him, so that Rufus wouldn't bark the next time he came around in the night."

"So that's why Rufus didn't alert us during the break-in!" exclaimed Lynn. "What a traitor! Imagine, letting himself be bribed with a little food!"

"But how did you find out that it was Martin and not Ste..."

Monica stopped suddenly, her face turning lobster-red.

"'Not Steven,' is that what you were gonna say?" asked Steven calmly.

Monica nodded unhappily. There was an awkward silence before Maria started talking again.

"Martin gave himself away. Remember when he came by and asked about boarding for his sister's horse yesterday morning? He said, 'Cause I assume you're not gonna keep sleeping in the stable every night'?"

Maria looked at the others. "How did he know that we'd slept in the stable, unless he'd been there in the night? We thought it was just an animal or something, because Rufus didn't bark, but then I realized that it must have been Martin. I suddenly remembered all the questions he had asked back in Amsterdam, and started putting two and two together. That is, Joanna helped, because the possibility of switched saddles had occurred to her too."

"That's right," said Joanna. "You see, I was writing about something similar in my new mystery novel. Only in my novel, it's about two backpacks and a fake bottom instead of riding saddles."

Joanna raked a hand through her hair. "I couldn't quite get it to fit, since the saddle was actually stolen and not replaced with the other one, so I gave up the idea. If I had known the details of Maria and Lynn's conversation with Martin at Easter, I might have understood sooner what the thieves were after."

"But what about the other burglaries in the area?" asked Thea. "Were Martin and his friend behind those too?"

David shook his head. "No, the police caught that gang last night. Caught them red-handed as they were breaking into a house. But they have nothing to do with 'our' case."

"Poor Mr. Olsen," said Thea's mother. "This will come as a terrible shock to him. He's always bragged about how wonderful Martin is and criticized other people's rude, misbehaving kids. Maybe he'll be a little less eager to judge others from now on."

"He won't be the only one!" Monica looked at Steven with tears in her eyes. "I thought it was you who had done it. Martin was saying all kinds of awful things about you, there were all those burglaries, and then suddenly you had a lot of money, and I had no idea about the football pool."

Her hand shook as she lifted her glass to take a sip of soda. "And yesterday I heard something you said on the phone. You were talking about a horse trailer, and I thought…"

"You thought I was going to break into the stable and steal one of the horses," finished Steven. "Right?"

"Yes," Monica whispered miserably. "Oh, Steven, can you forgive me? I can't believe I actually suspected you of doing something like that!"

"I can," said Steven calmly. "When I think about all the terrible things I did before, I don't blame you one bit for suspecting me. I would have done the same if I was in your shoes."

Monica stared at him in disbelief. "You mean it? You're not angry with me? I feel like the world's meanest sister!"

"Don't! Everyone makes mistakes now and then." Steven smiled. "Come here and give your big brother a hug, and then we'll be friends again, okay? Friends who trust each other."

Monica's face lit up. She jumped up and hugged Steven so hard he begged for his life.

"Help! Don't kill me! You're strangling me!" he whimpered, and they all started laughing. "You should have been here earlier tonight," he said after Monica had let go. "Then you would have seen some really suspicious behavior on my part. I came sneaking into the farmyard in order to smuggle something into the stable, but just as I rounded the corner, I walked right into Lynn. You should have seen her face!"

"You almost scared me to death," Lynn said with a laugh. "There we were, watching the crooks being taken away in the police car, and as I turn around I run right into a mysterious figure carrying some huge thingy in his arms!"

"You were here when Martin was arrested?" Monica looked at her brother in surprise. "What were you doing here in the middle of the night, anyway?"

"Well, why don't you go outside and see for yourself?" Steven smiled secretively. "Then you may also get an explanation for those mysterious phone calls that you were eavesdropping on!"

Monica didn't need to be told twice. She rushed out the door and ran to the stable. When she got inside, she stopped and stared. Cindy's stall had been decorated with colorful garlands and on the wall was a big poster with a sign that read, *To Monica! Happy Birthday! Sorry I didn't have time to wrap your gift, but I hope you like it anyway. Love, Steven.*

"I'm dreaming!" said Monica. "This isn't happening. It's impossible." She pinched herself hard on the arm. Ouch! It hurt. So she must be awake. With a shout of joy, she ran over to Cindy and threw her arms around the beautiful horse's neck. Cindy snorted and stroked her soft muzzle against

Monica's cheek.

"Oh, this is going too far!" said a sudden, humorous voice. "Now she's trying to strangle the horse too!"

Monica turned around. There was Steven with a big grin on his face. "Is it safe to assume that those horrible screams of yours mean that you like your present? I had planned to give you a pink teddy bear, but unfortunately they were all out!"

"Do I like it?" Monica threw her arms around her brother's neck, and gave him another bear hug. "It's the most wonderful gift I've ever gotten in my whole life! And I was so unhappy when I heard that Thomas had sold Cindy."

"Well, you mentioned that Thomas wasn't very interested in horses anymore, so I figured it couldn't hurt to ask if he might consider selling Cindy. I managed to get his cell phone number and called him. We talked several times, actually. It was one of those conversations that you overheard. Thomas wondered if I needed a horse trailer, but I'd already decided to keep Cindy here."

Steven laughed. "Thomas was really sorry he couldn't be here to see your face when you discovered that Cindy was yours, so I had to promise to give him a full report."

"Why don't you take a picture of Cindy and me with your phone to send to him, then," said Monica, and she put her arms around Cindy's neck again. "It'll be a long time before I stop smiling."

"Good idea!" Steven took out his cell phone and started taking pictures. "This one is good."

He located Thomas's number and sent the photo.

"This is just wonderful!" Monica sighed happily. "It's great that Cindy gets to stay where she is. And I get to spend time with

Lynn and the others every day."

"Yes. As a matter of fact, all day and all night for the next two weeks!"

Monica gave a start at the sound of Lynn's voice behind her.

"All day and all night? What do you mean?" Monica looked at her, puzzled.

"I can explain," said Monica's mother, who had just entered the stable, followed by the rest of the party. She embraced her daughter and gave her a warm hug. "As you may have gathered, Steven won a lot more money than he first let on. He kept it a secret because he wanted to surprise you on your birthday, and he had a surprise in store for me too! He and I are going on a two-week vacation to Greece, and while we're gone, you get to stay here with Lynn. Does that sound okay with you? Lynn and her parents say they'll be happy to have you."

Then her mother said teasingly. "But of course, if you'd rather lie on a Greek beach and suntan, we can arrange that too..."

"As if!" Monica was so overjoyed she didn't know what to say or do. "You know perfectly well what I want!" She stroked Cindy lovingly on the muzzle. "This is the best birthday, or rather, birthday night, I've ever had! I feel like the luckiest, happiest girl in the whole world!"

"And we're going to have so much fun this summer!" said Thea. "We can go riding..."

"...without being spied on by creepy

gangsters!" added Lynn.

"Yeah, and now we can finally make that jumping course we were planning to build, and have our very own gymkhana!" finished Monica. She was still grinning from ear to ear. "It'll be so cool!"

"You bet..." laughed Maria. "... not just cool, mega cool! Especially if we bring a bunch of good food!"

"Woof!" said Rufus.

THE END